THE SPECTER OF COMMUNISM

ALSO BY MELVYN P. LEFFLER

The Elusive Quest: America's Pursuit of European Stability and French Security, 1919–1933

A Preponderance of Power: National Security, the Truman Administration, and the Cold War

THE SPECTER OF COMMUNISM:

The United States and the Origins of the Cold War, 1917–1953

MELVYN P.
LEFFLER

A CRITICAL ISSUE

HILL AND WANG • NEW YORK
a division of Farrar, Straus and Giroux

Hill and Wang
A division of Farrar, Straus and Giroux
18 West 18th Street, New York 10011

Distributed in Canada by Douglas & McIntyre Ltd.
Printed in the United States of America
First edition, 1994

Library of Congress Cataloging-in-Publication Data
Leffler, Melvyn P., 1945–
The specter of communism : the United States and the origins of the Cold War, 1917–1953 / Melvyn P. Leffler ; consulting editor, Eric Foner.—1st ed.
p. cm.
Includes bibliographical references (p.) and index.
Hardcover ISBN-13: 978-0-8090-8791-4 (cloth)
Hardcover ISBN-10: 0-8090-8791-X (cloth)
Paperback ISBN-13: 978-0-8090-1574-0 (paper)
Paperback ISBN-10: 0-8090-1574-9 (paper)
1. Anti-communist movements—United States—History—20th century. 2. Cold War. 3. United States—Foreign relations—20th century. 4. United States—Foreign relations—Soviet Union. 5. Soviet Union—Foreign relations—United States. I. Foner, Eric. II. Title.

E744 .L432 1994
327.73—dc20

94013419

Designed by Fritz Metsch

www.fsgbooks.com

17 19 21 22 20 18

FOR

VINCENT J. KORAN

Preface and Acknowledgments

The Cold War dominated international relations for almost a half century after the end of World War II. For many Americans the preoccupation with Communism was not new; it had existed since the Bolshevik Revolution in 1917. Yet ideological hostility was not translated into a sense of mortal danger until Soviet armies helped defeat Nazi Germany and occupied much of Eastern Europe. The Cold War took shape when a sense of ideological rivalry merged with a fear of Soviet power. In this book I examine why and how this process occurred.

The fusion of ideological competition with geostrategic threat made American officials keenly sensitive to the vulnerability of their domestic political and economic institutions. In their view, configurations of power in the international system had a significant bearing on whether they could preserve individual liberties and a private market economy at home. During the years between the world wars, the Soviet Union had not been capable of exerting a decisive influence on the balance of power in Europe and Asia, and American attention tended either to be indifferent to political developments in these regions or, more usually, to focus on the potential strength of Germany and Japan. These attitudes were transformed by the experiences of the late 1930s and by the changes in the international system wrought by World War II itself.

After 1945, American policymakers were afraid not so much of the prospect of premeditated Soviet military aggression as of Soviet capabilities to capitalize on postwar vacuums of power in

Germany and Japan, socioeconomic dislocation in Europe, civil war in China, and decolonization in the Third World. Should these developments play into Soviet hands, the Kremlin would gain a position of preponderance in Eurasia akin to the position sought by the Axis powers (Germany, Italy, and Japan) on the eve of World War II. In this work I show that the lessons of the 1930s cast a huge shadow over postwar foreign policies. These lessons were not simply that appeasement did not work nor that exports were the key to prosperity, but that configurations of power abroad were critical to the maintenance of a free political economy at home. American officials had concluded as early as 1940 that they could not live in a world dominated by totalitarian nations, even if those powers refrained from attacking the United States.

The sophisticated thinking of Washington officials about power, freedom, and prosperity does not alone explain why the United States waged the Cold War as it did. Anti-Communism resonated with the American people. It provided a framework for understanding a complicated world with which few Americans had much experience. Anti-Communism also could be used and manipulated by a wide variety of groups and interests to serve more limited domestic goals. In the pages that follow I try to outline how different business, religious, patriotic, and sectional groups vigorously supported the Cold War, even though they sometimes demonstrated scant interest in the Soviet Union itself. Politicians grasped the appeal of anti-Communism—Joe McCarthy more than anyone. But other leaders realized that the Cold War itself could go too far; that in the struggle to combat Communism the United States itself could become more like the enemy, could become a garrison state.

Officials in Washington sought not only to generate a Cold War consensus at home but also to organize most of the world into an American-led orbit. Gradually, the United States assumed an unprecedented leadership role in the international system. Policymakers tried to rebuild Western Europe, co-opt the strength of Germany and Japan, and integrate the industrial core of Eurasia with its underdeveloped periphery in Southeast Asia, the Middle East, and North Africa. These efforts were extraordinarily complex, and American officials sought to achieve their goals not simply by forcing other countries to do what the United States wanted, but also by seeking to accommodate their needs and interests. Unprecedented power and wealth afforded the United States an unusual advantage. Sometimes policymakers used this leverage wisely; sometimes foolishly.

The overriding goal of the United States was to contain the spread of Soviet power and Communist influence. Whether policymakers in Washington correctly assessed the adversary's intentions and capabilities is a fascinating subject. In this book I incorporate findings from Russian, East European, and Chinese archives and memoirs. The new materials often provide revealing glimpses of the perceptions, fears, and aims of America's foes, even of Stalin himself. I try to show how the men in the Kremlin defined their goals, interpreted American initiatives, and interacted with fellow Communists abroad.

I am greatly indebted to many friends, colleagues, and graduate students who helped me with this book. James Lewis, Laura Belmonte, Michael O'Brien, and Andy Lewis did valuable research. When I was a fellow at the Nobel Peace Institute in Norway, Geir Lundestad, Odd Arne Westad, Vladimir Zhubok, and Patrick Stewart gave the first draft a careful reading and offered many constructive suggestions. So did several of my friends and colleagues at the University of Virginia, including Ed Ayers, Steve Schuker, Tico Braun, Nelson Lichtenstein, Brian Balogh, and Colleen Doody. I asked Bob McMahon and Frank Costigliola for their comments, and they both provided extremely thoughtful advice, for which I am most grateful. My wife, Phyllis, read the manuscript in the final stages and prevailed upon me yet again to cut, clarify, and make accessible to the reader the richness and excitement of the most recent scholarly research on the Cold War.

This book is dedicated to Vincent J. Koran, my friend and father-in-law. Beginning in the 1960s, we argued over Castro's revolution, the war in Vietnam, the civil rights movement, and the legacy of the New Deal. No conservative I knew was more intelligent, more persistent, and more imaginative in his arguments. No friend I had was more tolerant and supportive of my work and our differences. He would have read this book and quibbled over every point. I miss him.

Contents

THE SPECTER OF COMMUNISM

(1)

THE BACKGROUND

1917–1941

FROM the beginning, there was an ideological clash. When the Bolsheviks seized power in Russia in November 1917, in the midst of World War I, they appealed to workers everywhere to overthrow their governments. "We summon you to this struggle, workers of all countries! There is no other way. The crimes of the ruling, exploiting classes in this war have been countless. These crimes cry out for revolutionary revenge."[1]

The Bolsheviks believed that their revolution in Russia would be crushed if they did not sue for peace, spark revolution abroad, and consolidate their victory at home. They appealed to the exhausted peoples of Europe to support their campaign for a peace without annexations and without indemnities, a peace based on the principle of self-determination for peoples everywhere. In December, the Council of People's Commissars appropriated two million rubles for the international revolutionary movement. The message was direct: "The workers' revolution calls upon the working classes of all countries to revolt."[2]

The Bolsheviks envisioned a classless society in a warless world. They talked of a vast expansion of democracy, a democracy for the poor and the powerless. They said they would abolish private property, allocate control of the workplace to the workers themselves, fairly distribute the fruits of production, and give the peasants the land on which they labored. Their rhetoric of peace and self-determination encoded a message to common people of all lands to rise up and empower themselves. The Bolsheviks wanted them to overturn an exploitative political and economic system that subjected them to the impersonal functioning of a marketplace economy and that forced them to wage war in behalf of capitalists seeking colonial markets, raw materials, and investment opportunities.

But profound disillusionment and social ferment in the warring countries did not lead to immediate revolutionary upheaval. Within weeks the Bolsheviks had to decide whether to sign a humiliating peace with Germany or to sustain the deadly struggle. Some Bolsheviks abhorred a separate peace, one that would make them accomplices of German imperialism. Notwithstanding the odds, they wanted to work for revolution abroad.

But V. I. Lenin, the leader of the Bolsheviks, rebuffed this line of reasoning. If the struggle persisted, he argued, the revolution would be crushed. Russian soldiers were deserting their military units in great numbers, and the German onslaught could not be stopped. A peace had to be signed with Germany so that the Bolsheviks could concentrate on defeating their domestic foes. "The hands of the Socialist government," Lenin remonstrated, "must be absolutely free for the job of vanquishing the bourgeoisie in our own country."[3]

Lenin exercised the decisive voice in support of signing the separate treaty with Germany, the Treaty of Brest-Litovsk. In March 1918 the Bolsheviks relinquished the Ukraine as well as Poland, Finland, Estonia, Latvia, Lithuania, and a slice of land (Kars) along the border with Turkey. These territories contained a substantial percentage of Russia's raw materials and industrial infrastructure, perhaps as much as three-quarters of its iron and steel, a quarter of its railway network, a quarter of its population, and a large share of its most fertile soil.

Lenin hoped he would gain the necessary time to develop an army, organize the economy, and defeat the multiple opponents who threatened from every direction. His position was desperate. Large parts of Russia were occupied by the Germans. National minorities were battling for local autonomy. Counterrevolutionary, or "White," forces were gathering momentum.

1. Russian Territorial Losses at Brest-Litovsk, 1918

Adapted by William L. Nelson from *Russia: A History of the Soviet Period*, by Woodford McClellan (Englewood Cliffs, N.J.: Prentice-Hall, 1990)

And, meanwhile, Russia's industrial economy was disintegrating. Hungry and disenchanted workers left the cities in great numbers. Angry and rebellious peasants refused to sell their crops for worthless currency.

The situation was chaotic. The Bolsheviks, like many of their domestic foes, were willing to take aid from any quarter. Despite the separate peace with the Kaiser, Lenin and his comrades did not feel secure. The Germans, in the midst of their gigantic offensive on the western front in France, continued to gobble up chunks of Russian territory along the Black and Crimean seas and supported separatist movements from the Baltic to the Caucasus. The Bolsheviks, therefore, solicited aid and assistance from Russia's former allies—the British, the French, and the Americans—even while they continued to iron out their treaty and trade arrangements with the Germans.

During the spring of 1918 Leon Trotsky, the commander of the Red army, and Georgi Chicherin, the commissar in charge of foreign affairs, met frequently with American and British diplomatic emissaries, military attachés, and philanthropic officials. In addition to seeking formal diplomatic recognition, they wanted food, military supplies, technical assistance, and credits. Bowing to an Allied request, they agreed that 70,000 Czech troops might travel east along the Trans-Siberian railroad to Vladivostok where they would cross the oceans and eventually join the battle on the western front. But Trotsky and Chicherin were not willing to resume the war against the Central Powers. And desperate to win the struggle on the home front, they indoctrinated and liberated German and Austrian prisoners of war, seeking to use them against their domestic foes.

The rhetoric and actions of the Bolsheviks ignited fear, revulsion, and uncertainty in Washington. The American secretary of state, Robert Lansing, abhorred Bolshevism. He saw it as a new form of despotism, a class despotism "subversive of the rights of man, and hostile to justice and liberty."[4] Appalled by the Bolsheviks' efforts to withdraw from the conflict, Lansing urged President Woodrow Wilson not to recognize the fledgling new regime. The United States, Lansing believed, should await the formation of "a strong and stable government founded on the principles of democracy and the equality of man," a government that would guarantee "every citizen of free Russia . . . the enjoyment of his inherent rights of life, liberty and the pursuit of happiness."[5]

The president agreed that the United States must exercise extreme caution. The Bolsheviks angered him. He was agitated by their repudiation of the debts of former Russian governments and by their removal of Allied war supplies from Archangel, a key port on the White Sea. Still more upsetting to Wilson was the Bolshevik dissolution of the Constituent Assembly, the most democratically elected body Russia had ever experienced. Garnering only 175 out of 715 seats in the Assembly, Lenin could not dominate it, so he decided to disband it. Although Trotsky argued that the principles of democracy had to be "trampled underfoot" for the "sake of the loftier principles of a social revolution," Wilson deemed Trotsky to be "absolutely untrustworthy" and was morally repulsed by Bolshevik contempt for majority rule.[6] Maintaining that the Bolsheviks did not represent the Russian people, Wilson was not inclined to recognize their government.

Bolshevik appeals to the war-wearied masses of Europe and their clamor for a peace without annexations and indemnities deeply troubled American officials. The president's advisors believed Wilson should not permit Lenin to monopolize this rhetoric. In their view, the Bolsheviks were using this language to lead the Russian people astray and to sign a separate peace with Germany. They urged Wilson to employ the same powerful message of peace and reform to revitalize flagging support for the war among the European allies, entice the Russians themselves to stay in the war, and prompt the German people to overthrow their government. These considerations inspired Wilson to offer his own vision of a peaceful world order in his Fourteen Points speech in January 1918, one of the most important messages he ever delivered. Wilson was not afraid of the Bolsheviks' revolutionary domestic program, for he was sure it would fail, but he worried that Bolshevik rhetoric would capture the imagination of European peoples, erode Allied support for the war, and open the possibility of a German victory.

In the spring of 1918 nothing influenced Wilson and his advisors more than the necessity of defeating the Germans and their partners. Lenin's willingness to sign a separate peace, trade with the enemy, and use German and Austrian prisoners of war repelled Wilson. The separate peace meant that Germany could redeploy dozens of divisions to the western front during a decisive moment in the conflict. A separate peace and the trade that ensued showed that Bolshevik Russia was willing to cede land and sell critical raw materials and foodstuffs to the enemy.

During March, April, and May of 1918, virtually every Allied assessment stressed the dangers that would ensue if an eastern front was not reopened. The military representatives on the Allied Supreme War Council believed that Germany was enhancing its war-making capabilities by requisitioning food supplies in the Ukraine and demanding shipments of wheat, butter, and fats from western Siberia. According to Allied intelligence reports, the Germans were struggling "to organize as large a part of the Russian Empire as possible as a friendly State . . . not only to draw upon its economic resources, but to transfer to the West a great part of the 47 Divisions which Germany still maintains on the Eastern front."[7]

The danger of a German-Soviet combination would be a recurrent nightmare over the next decades. To thwart this prospect in 1918, the French, the British, and the Japanese wanted to intervene militarily and reestablish an eastern front in Russia. Had the Bolsheviks been willing and able to do this on their own, the Allies might have worked with them, at least temporarily, despite their ideological antipathy. But the Allies did not think that the Bolsheviks would cooperate, because any collaboration would prompt the Germans to crush the Bolshevik regime. Intent on preventing the "military and economic exploitation of Russia by Germany," the British and the French pressed the United States to intervene militarily.[8]

Wilson agonized. He viewed the Bolsheviks with contempt.

But he did not fear their power, and he did not expect them to survive unless they wrapped themselves in the cause of nationalism and the defense of Mother Russia. He opposed intervention for a long time because he distrusted the Allies, knowing they were animated, at least in part, by their desires to safeguard their investments, preserve their empires, and, in the case of Japan, annex parts of Russia.

Wilson relented when the Czech troops, moving east on the Trans-Siberian railroad, became locked in battle with local Bolshevik forces. To everyone's surprise, the Czechs quickly took control of the railroad line, linked up with White contingents in the area, and captured much of western Siberia. This happened as German artillery approached the outskirts of Paris and Premier Georges Clemenceau toyed with the idea of abandoning the French capital. The British remonstrated yet again, and Wilson now agreed that intervention was "an urgent necessity both to save the Czecho-Slovaks and to take advantage of an opportunity of gaining control of Siberia for the Allies which may never return."[9]

Wilson sent 7,000 U.S. troops to Siberia and smaller numbers to Archangel as a wartime expedient. He sought to thwart German co-optation of Russian resources, safeguard Allied military supplies, and prevent a total concentration of German forces on the western front. Japanese, British, and French contingents intervened in much larger numbers, and one of Wilson's motives was to monitor their behavior and balance their influence.

The intrusion of the Allies into Russian territory, their collaboration with different factions battling the Red armies, and their blockade of Russian waterways confirmed Bolshevik assumptions that all the belligerents in the conflict were imperialist aggressors determined to overthrow the only socialist state. In turn, the Bolsheviks increased their assistance to the Germans, even as the Kaiser's armies retreated and defeat was imminent.

The armistice on the western front in November 1918 should have ended the Allied military intervention in Russia, but it did not. The Red menace seemed greater in the aftermath of war

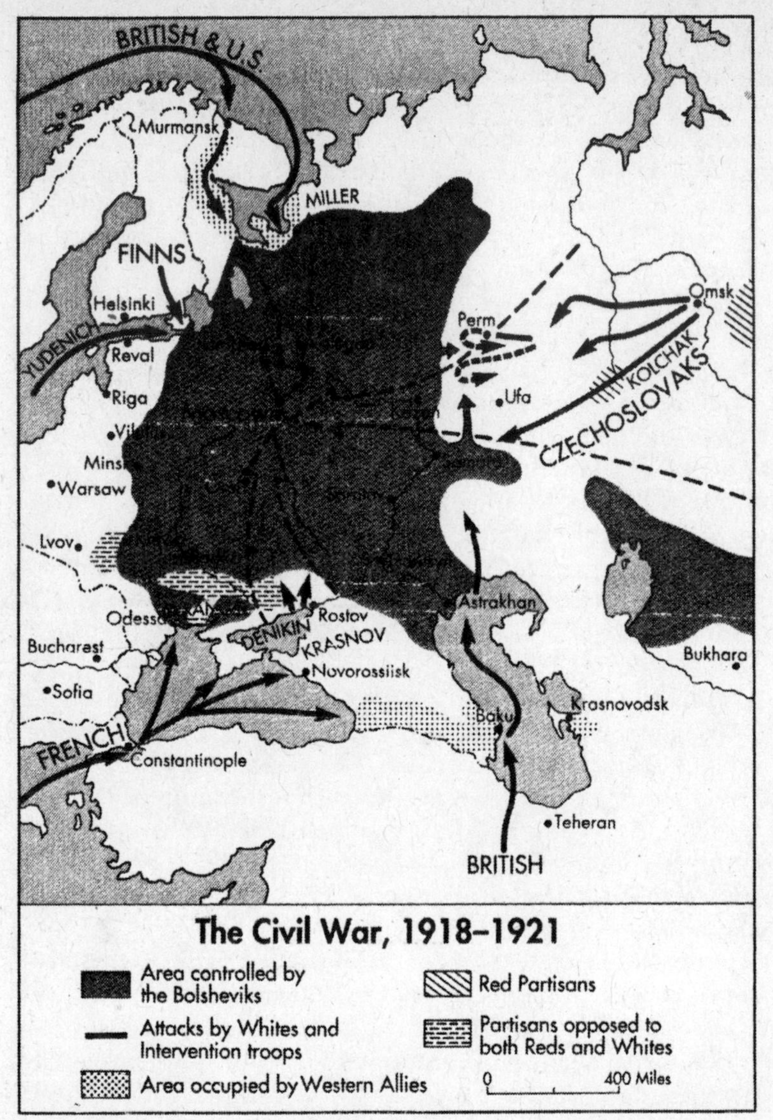

2. The Civil War, 1918–1921

Adapted by William L. Nelson from *Russia and the Soviet Union: An Historical Introduction*, by John M. Thompson (New York: Charles Scribner's Sons, 1986)

than ever before. As the guns quieted and soldiers returned home, famine and unemployment spread. All through east-central Europe peasants sought land; workers looked for jobs; and subject peoples struggled for nationhood and territory, often at the expense of one another. While the triumphant Allies worked on peace treaties that the vanquished nations would be forced to sign, the blockade of Germany persisted and so did the hardship and hunger of the German people. And inside Russia, Lenin, Trotsky, and their comrades waged a brutal civil war while simultaneously repelling a Polish attack and organizing the Third International, the Comintern, to institutionalize the gospel of revolution abroad.

The peacemakers in Paris were alarmed by the ferment and upheaval that racked postwar Europe. Wilson grew irascible as he and his colleagues disputed the terms of peace and prolonged the treaty-making process. "The world was on fire," he declared on March 25, 1919, and "every minute lost assisted the forces of unrest."[10] His ideological animus toward Bolshevism grew as he received reports of the ferocity of the civil war in Russia and the spread of revolutionary fervor abroad. "That ugly, poisonous thing called Bolshevism," he told the Democratic National Committee during a brief return to Washington in February 1919, fed on people's doubts and despair.[11] Wilson knew that Bolshevism's strength rested in its great appeal to demoralized and starving people. He feared that a tough treaty would radicalize the German people and drive them into the hands of the German Bolsheviks.

This seemed to be happening elsewhere. When Romania seized additional Hungarian land in March 1919, right-wing Hungarian politicians handed power to Béla Kun, a Communist. Kun rallied support by defending Hungarian territory, confirming Wilson's assumptions that Bolshevism thrived on the despair and disillusionment of peoples accustomed to traditional forms of national aggrandizement and autocratic rule.

Wilson, however, was convinced that military force could not cure the Bolshevik virus. "The only real protection against it," he said, "was food and industry" coupled with a just peace and a League of Nations.[12] Wilson wanted to lift the blockade against Germany and provide the new liberal government with food and raw materials, so economic life could begin anew. Allied troops in Russia, he thought, should also be withdrawn. "I believe in letting them [the Russians] work out their own salvation," he told a British friend in November 1918, "even though they wallow in anarchy a while."[13]

Bolshevik ideology and practice remained repugnant to Wilson, but, devoid of a power base, Russian Bolshevism posed no threat worthy of military intervention. If peace was restored and the processes of recovery resumed, Wilson believed, "Bolshevism would collapse." The president was more fearful that an angry, revenge-minded, and imperial Russia might supplant the Bolsheviks and unite with a resurgent Germany. "There was nothing in the treaty with Germany," he noted, "to prevent the Germans from forming a powerful industrial and commercial union with Russia."[14]

Wilson wanted to win the loyalty and affection of European peoples. He wanted them to emulate the American experience and adopt the principles and values of a free political economy, an economy of liberal capitalism. Bolshevism represented the antithesis of everything he believed in. But since the Russian Bolsheviks posed no strategic threat in themselves, the way to deal with Bolshevism, whether it be Russian or Hungarian or German, was to allay the conditions of poverty and inequality on which it thrived. The United States and its allies could do this most effectively through aid and assistance.

Wilson was not alone in believing this. His advisors staunchly opposed French and British plans for a large postwar invasion of Russia. Most illuminating were the views of Herbert C. Hoover. During the 1920s, Hoover became a prominent Republican, an influential secretary of commerce, and then president of the United States. But during World War I and its immediate aftermath Hoover took charge of all relief efforts in Europe and was a key advisor to President Wilson. Hoover observed revolutionary eruptions throughout the Baltic states, Eastern Europe, and the Balkans. He understood that, amid the prevailing misery, the appeal of Bolshevism was immense. "Socialism and Communism," Hoover noted, had embraced "the claim to speak for all the downtrodden, to alone bespeak human sympathy and to alone present remedies, to be the lone voice of liberalism."[15]

Like Wilson, Hoover appreciated the yearnings of European peoples. But he believed Communism was a false philosophy: misguided, evil, and inhumane. From the Baltic to the Balkans, Hoover received reports of Communist perfidy, extortion, and murder. He knew they alone were not guilty of such actions; he knew their opponents often acted as cruelly and arbitrarily as the Bolsheviks. But he was nonetheless sickened by their plunder and executions. Remembering the situation in Latvia, where the Communists briefly held control in the spring of 1919, Hoover believed that "literally hundreds of innocent people were executed daily without trial in a sadistic orgy of blood. . . . Clergymen, doctors, teachers, young girls, were taken to prison and mowed down by machine guns. . . . Deaths from starvation and other causes were so many that coffins could not be provided, and bodies by the hundreds were dumped into trenches."[16]

Hoover detested Bolshevism because it was economically unsound and politically repressive. The Bolsheviki, he wrote Wilson in March 1919, "most certainly represent a minority in every country where they are in control, and as such they constitute a tyranny that is the negation of democracy, for democracy, as I see it, must rest on the execution of the will of the majority expressed by free and unfettered suffrage."[17] Because the Bolsheviks also ignored the axiom that productivity rested on the stimulus of self interest as well as altruism, Hoover did not think they could respond to humanity's needs any better than their autocratic predecessors. The Reds and the Whites, in his view, were equally nefarious.

But Hoover, like Wilson, did not champion military intervention to crush Bolshevism. He favored using food and aid to blunt its spread. Through the relief agencies he controlled and the railroad transport he coordinated, Hoover allocated food and raw materials to movements and governments he supported and withheld assistance from those he opposed. In Hungary, for example, he denied food to Béla Kun's revolutionary government and helped to overthrow it in August 1919.

Hoover wished to apply similar policies to Russia. Like Wilson, he did not think that the Bolsheviks constituted a long-term threat to the United States. They would muster support only if they wrapped themselves in the mantle of nationalism, defending Russia against outside interlopers. Hence Hoover wanted to withdraw U.S. troops from Russia and deliver aid to the Russian people without recognizing the Bolsheviks. He believed that relief would enhance the image of the United States and win sympathy for the American system. There was no need to do more than this, because it was most important to complete the peace treaty with Germany, establish the League of Nations, and restore the processes of economic recovery. Once recovery began elsewhere in Europe, Hoover assumed, Bolshevism was likely to collapse inside Russia.

While the peacemakers were arguing over the treaty with Germany and pondering how to stop the spread of Bolshevism, the Red Scare erupted in the United States. The Russian Revolution and the Communist risings in central and Eastern Europe exhilarated American radicals and frightened their conservative foes. Strikes, bombings, and parades on May Day 1919 ignited fears that the Communist menace was invading American shores. Wilson had thought that the "American Negro returning from abroad would be our greatest medium in conveying bolshevism to America," but most Americans identified aliens, recent immigrants, and radical unions as the greater threat.[18]

The war bred an aroused nationalism and accustomed Americans to think about sabotage and subversion. Patriotic groups, veterans organizations, business associations, and the Catholic Church wanted to root out every vestige of domestic Communism and many other forms of radicalism as well. Thirty-five states passed sedition laws, banned displays of red flags, and investigated radicals. In Washington, A. Mitchell Palmer, Wilson's new attorney general, created a unit to hunt subversives and placed it under a recent law-school graduate, J. Edgar Hoover. In January 1920, Palmer's agents arrested over 6,000 suspected Communists in twenty-three states. Hundreds were deported, often on the flimsiest evidence.

Most Americans were more concerned with Bolshevism at home than with Bolshevism abroad. Since the Bolsheviks were widely depicted as German agents (as a result of their withdrawal from the conflict), it was easy to call them traitors. Since they believed in class rather than nation, they could be condemned for lacking patriotism and for betraying American values and institutions. Since in Russia they immediately liberalized divorce, attacked the church, and decriminalized adultery, they could be denounced as godless atheists. Bolshevism, said *The New York Times*, meant "chaos, wholesale murder, the complete destruction of civilization."[19] Such rhetoric resonated throughout America. Businessmen used it to crush unions; fundamentalist preachers used it to summon the faithful; white Anglo-Saxon Americans used it to limit immigration; and southern and midwestern racists used it to intimidate African Americans, Jews, and Catholics.

Even President Wilson indulged in Red-baiting. Although he said he was not afraid of Bolshevism in America, in his campaign for Senate ratification of the Treaty of Versailles and the League of Nations he could not resist labeling his opponents Bolsheviks. He warned against the "poison . . . running in the veins of the world" and the "apostles of Lenin in our midst." He linked the ongoing police strike in Boston to events in Russia and he equated American radicals with Russian Bolsheviks.[20]

In American politics, liberals as well as conservatives would brand their enemies as Communists. This rhetoric appealed to the American people because they abhorred Bolshevik ideology and Communist practices even while they felt little threat from Bolshevism in Russia. Most Americans, in fact, supported Wilson's withdrawal of troops from Russia in mid-1920, and even many businessmen called for the lifting of the blockade.

Wilson, however, never did formally recognize the Bolsheviks.

His ideological opposition mounted after he was afflicted with a terrible stroke in September 1919. And although Robert Lansing, the rigidly anti-Bolshevik secretary of state, had left office, his successor, Bainbridge Colby, issued a statement in August 1920 that set policy for the next thirteen years. The United States, Colby declared, would not recognize the Bolsheviks, because they were not representative of the will of the Russian people, because they were dedicated to fomenting revolution abroad through the Comintern, and because they rejected the fundamental principles of international relations by repudiating debts and ignoring the sanctity of contracts.

American policies disappointed the Bolsheviks. During 1919 and 1920, they looked to the United States for aid, trade, and recognition. They hoped to split off the United States from the other allies and to procure supplies that were critical for winning the civil war and alleviating starvation. Even after U.S. intervention, Lenin extended favored treatment to American business interests and exempted U.S. firms operating in Russia from nationalization. Believing that the United States needed Russian raw materials and fearing the growth of German and Japanese power, Soviet leaders thought they could entice the Wilson administration into a working relationship.

But talk of interdependence did not mean that the Russian Communists had abandoned their perception of threat. Foreign intervention on Russian soil and aid, albeit limited aid, to their opponents by Britain, France, Japan, Romania, Czechoslovakia, Finland, Turkey, and the United States confirmed Bolshevik suspicions that foreign imperialists would do what they could to crush the workers' revolution. The Polish invasion of Soviet Russia in 1920, with French support, reinforced these views.

Lenin's focus on safeguarding the revolution inside Russia, however, did not betoken a fundamental shift in goals. "Until the final victory of socialism throughout the world," he told Communist party secretaries in November 1920, the Bolsheviks must "exploit the contradictions and antagonisms between the two imperialisms, between the two systems of capitalist States, inciting them one against the other." By making concessions to one form of imperialism, even humiliating concessions as had been the case with Brest-Litovsk, "[we] fenced ourselves off from persecution by both imperialisms. . . . But as soon as we are strong enough to fight the whole of capitalism," Lenin boasted, "we shall at once take it by the neck. Our strength is growing and very quickly too."[21]

Lenin's boasts did not frighten U.S. officials. Peasant disaffection, worker revolts, and minority uprisings continued to beleaguer Bolshevik leaders even after they defeated their opponents. The new Soviet state, moreover, was devoid of the lands that the czars had annexed in previous centuries, including Finland, Latvia, Estonia, Lithuania, most of eastern Poland, a small part of Romania (Bessarabia), and Kars in northeastern Turkey. The economy was in pitiful shape. Industrial production was less than 15 percent of what it had been in 1913. In 1921, the yield of all crops was around 40 percent of the output in prewar years. Famine stalked large parts of Russia, killing between three and five million people and scarring the lives of perhaps another thirty million. Inflation was rampant, consumer goods scarce. People dressed in old uniforms, draperies, and tablecloths.

The new Bolshevik Russia did not inspire fear; it inspired pity, contempt, and hope. In 1922 Herbert Hoover, now the secretary of commerce in the Republican administration of Warren Harding, organized a major nongovernmental effort to distribute food and allay suffering. Hoover and the Republicans thought that assistance would enable Americans to take the lead in the reconstruction of Russia when Communism faltered. Lenin's New Economic Policy in the 1920s, which reinstituted some forms of private property and market exchange, offered hope that Russia might be changing. With the encouragement of Lenin and his successors, a few American businessmen invested in Russia; thousands of U.S. engineers went there to exercise their talents; General Electric built a huge dam; and Henry Ford helped create the automobile and truck industry. The U.S. government permitted private investment and trade, even while it frowned upon loans and eschewed recognition.

American officials, like those in Western European capitals, were eager to reintegrate Russia into the world economy. After World War I, European countries needed Russian markets and raw materials in order to revive their industries and expand their exports. Lenin welcomed mutually beneficial commercial relations. In early 1922, the former Allies invited Soviet representatives to an international economic meeting at Genoa. During this conference German and Bolshevik diplomats met at nearby Rapallo and struck a deal to forgive past financial claims, establish diplomatic ties, and begin secret military arrangements. Rapallo angered the French and frightened the British, who decided (when a Labour government was formed in 1924) to normalize relations with the Bolshevik regime in Moscow. Fearful of the inroads that the Germans and the British might make, Republican officials supported private American initiatives in Bolshevik Russia.

The unsuccessful attempt to integrate Russia into the world economy was one small aspect of the American approach to European affairs in the 1920s. Republican officials rejected the League of Nations, rebuffed overtures to guarantee French security, refused to cancel the war debts, and maintained high tariffs. But they were not indifferent to events in the Old World. They sought to promote European stability through the limitation of armaments, the elimination of discriminatory trade practices, and the mobilization of private capital. They believed stability was prerequisite to prosperity and peace. If stability was achieved, Bolshevism would flounder because its roots were conflict, poverty, and inequality.

But the government of the United States did not pay a great deal of attention to the Bolshevik regime in Soviet Russia, because the latter was rather powerless. At the time of the Washington Disarmament Conference in 1921–22, the General Board of the Navy acknowledged the potential strength of the Russian army, but noted that disorganization was so pervasive and the prospects for stabilization so minimal that it wasn't necessary to give much thought to Russia for the foreseeable life of an arms limitation treaty. During the 1920s, in fact, the United States made no war plans against the new Union of

Soviet Socialist Republics. Great Britain and Japan occupied the attention of U.S. war planners, but Soviet Russia did not.

Republican officials, while not afraid of the Kremlin's strength, had no desire to recognize the Bolshevik regime. It was like "having a wicked and disgraceful neighbor," Hoover recollected in his memoirs. "We did not attack him, but we did not give him a certificate of character by inviting him into our homes."[22] Since Communists confiscated property, repudiated debts, violated the sanctity of contracts, and fomented revolution in other lands, the American government would not establish formal diplomatic ties.

Anti-Bolshevism was institutionalized in the U.S. State Department. In 1924 the Russian and East European sections were merged into a single division of Eastern European Affairs and placed under Robert F. Kelley. An Irish Catholic, trained by Russian émigrés and attracted to prerevolutionary Russia, Kelley detested the Bolsheviks and demanded that his subordinates share his view. He insisted that young foreign service officers like George F. Kennan and Charles Bohlen receive language training in Paris and Berlin, primarily by anti-Bolshevik émigrés, and he forbade them from spending their summers in the Soviet Union. Kelley believed the Bolsheviks were militantly expansionist. Through listening posts that he established in the Baltic capitals, Kelley closely monitored Soviet subversive activities around the world. Ignoring economic and social conditions inside other nations, he and his colleagues detected the Bolshevik hand behind unrest in Mexico, Nicaragua, Cuba, Spain, and Greece. In contrast, they began to look favorably upon rightist movements that promised stability and contested Bolshevik influence.

During the 1920s, no official in the American government thought more conceptually about the Bolshevik threat than Hoover. The specter of Communism, in his view, was ideological and moral, not geopolitical or strategic. "Five or six great social philosophies," he believed, were struggling "for ascendancy." There was "American Individualism," and it competed with Communism, socialism, syndicalism, and autocracy.[23]

Hoover was not afraid of the challenge. He extolled the

American system of "progressive individualism." It was based on private property, free enterprise, a marketplace economy, equal opportunity for every individual, free elections, and limited government. The system, Hoover readily acknowledged, had its flaws: business fluctuations, uncertainty of employment, arrogant employers, irresponsible unions, and a spirit of lawlessness. But he was sure it was superior to its competitors. While claiming that Communism in Soviet Russia proved itself with blood and misery, Hoover said that the free political economy of the United States stimulated science and technology, fostered individual achievement, generated economic growth, promoted social welfare, and ameliorated the standard of living of all the people—not just a single class. Running for president in 1928, he declared that Republican policies had created a "New Day," an unrivaled prosperity in an emerging capitalist commonwealth.

In Bolshevik Russia, Lenin's New Economic Policy gradually gave way to a command economy based on five-year plans, forced industrialization, and the collectivization of agriculture. Fierce wrangling among Lenin's heirs led to a devastating power struggle in which Joseph Stalin emerged as the dominant leader of a repressive state bureaucracy and party apparatus. After seeing the failure of revolutions abroad and watching the massacre of Chinese Communists, Stalin focused on developing socialism in one country, the Soviet Union. Wars between capitalist and Communist states, he thought, were inevitable, but they had to be postponed.

Communist predictions that a great crisis was brewing in the Western capitalist world proved true in 1929, when the New York stock market crashed and the Great Depression began. Agricultural prices fell, factory output slumped, world trade contracted, private banks folded, and the international financial system collapsed. Tens of millions of people lost their jobs, their farms, and their savings. The depression struck Germany, Japan, and the United States most harshly, but it engulfed all nations and engendered despair everywhere.

Economic hardship discredited American individualism, bour-

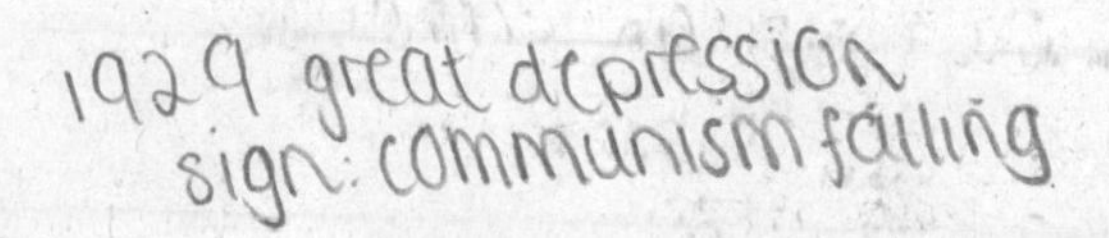

geois democracy, and liberal capitalism. Across Europe and Asia, distraught and sullen people were attracted to radical movements on the political right and left. Nazism and fascism gained millions of adherents, while Communism also assumed a new luster. In the United States, many Americans believed that their gloom and resignation contrasted sharply with the hopefulness and purposefulness in the Soviet Union. Thousands of Americans visited Russia in the early 1930s, and many returned home with favorable accounts. Ignoring or discounting the human toll of collectivization, they regarded the rational planning of a command economy as superior to the vagaries and hardships of a private marketplace economy and a free enterprise system. New initiatives seemed imperative when circumstances appeared dire. Repudiating Hoover's "New Day," Americans voted the Republicans out of office and elected Franklin D. Roosevelt president of the United States in 1932.

The Great Depression heartened Stalin. Declaring that it sharpened the contradictions inherent in world capitalism, Stalin predicted that capitalist rivalries would grow, as would the antagonisms between imperial powers and colonial peoples. The masses, he believed, would reject social democracy and turn toward Communism.

Stalin recognized, however, that Bolshevik Russia was still relatively weak. Japan's aggression in Manchuria in late 1931 and early 1932 worried him. The Japanese might follow this invasion with efforts to seize Russia's Pacific maritime provinces or parts of Siberia, territory they had eyed during the Great War but had grudgingly abandoned. Stalin did not yet order Comintern parties to establish united fronts with other democratic parties, but he repeatedly called for peace, trade, and economic relations with capitalist countries. He needed time to build his workers' paradise. If war erupted too soon and if fighting among capitalist nations prompted an attack on the Bolshevik motherland, his regime might crumble.

Roosevelt, too, faced unprecedented challenges. He inaugurated a "New Deal" to reinvigorate the American economy and alleviate suffering among the American people. He envisioned

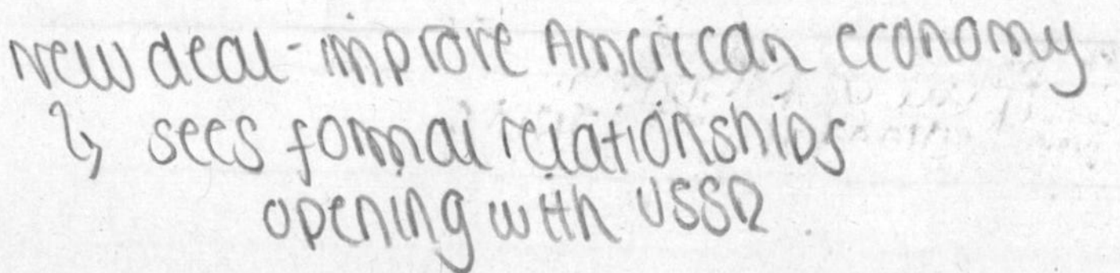

a new role for the government to guarantee the private banking system, to become the employer of last resort, to regulate the vagaries of the private marketplace, and to reform and resuscitate liberal capitalism. While focusing on domestic matters, he broke with the past and opened formal diplomatic relations with the USSR in 1933.

Economic and geopolitical factors pushed Roosevelt in this direction. By 1933, U.S. exports had dropped by almost 40 percent, and Russian markets beckoned. With Japan on the rampage, a Soviet-American rapprochement seemed like a prudent warning to Tokyo to change its behavior. Roosevelt, of course, demanded that the Russians acknowledge their war debts, forswear the promotion of revolution in the United States, and respect the religious freedom of Americans inside the Soviet Union.

Stalin had little trouble saying he would comply with these conditions. But his commitments were simply a matter of expediency. The debts, for example, were those of the czarist government, for which the Communist regime eschewed responsibility. Stalin believed that the United States and other Western nations should stop pontificating about the sanctity of contracts. By intervening in the revolution, he said, they had committed "acts of robbery" and forfeited the right to speak of international law and international obligations.[24]

But self-interest impelled both the Soviet and the American governments to overlook past grievances and to try to harmonize their policies. Stalin, in particular, acknowledged the deteriorating international situation. In January 1933, the Nazis came to power in Germany. Their rhetoric was viciously anti-Soviet and anti-Communist. Nazi dictator Adolf Hitler hunted and slaughtered domestic Communists. Stalin, seeing the Germans rearm and the Japanese consolidate their hold in Manchuria, knew his country was no match for the enemies that surrounded him. He brought the Soviet Union into the League of Nations. Soviet Foreign Minister Maksim Litvinov became one of the most eloquent exponents of collective security. Through the Comintern, the Kremlin instructed Communist parties abroad to cooperate in popular-front alliances with other antifascist groups. Their primary loyalty, Stalin insisted, was to the Soviet Union: "The triumph of the revolution in the USSR is the triumph of the revolution throughout the world."[25]

Stalin hastily sought to rearm his country. Millions perished from the dislocation, starvation, and persecution that accompanied forced collectivization, heavy industrialization, and rapid rearmament. Stalin's lust for power was matched only by his anxiety over the fate of his regime and the survival of the Bolshevik experiment. Obsessively suspicious, he purged his former comrades, his generals, and members of his scientific and technocratic elite. Everywhere he saw traitors and enemies. In fact, the victims of his purges had no links to foreign governments, but beyond its borders the Soviet Union did have powerful foes.

Roosevelt and his advisors watched events across the oceans carefully. Since the United States still remained outside the League of Nations and was far away from the world's most incendiary trouble spots, policymakers hoped to remain unembroiled in future hostilities. In the mid-1930s, they assumed that, among the many nations competing for power, no single country in Europe or Asia was likely to gain preeminent strength. The international system appeared multipolar. Its very multipolarity seemed to guarantee U.S. security. Congress passed neutrality legislation that barred loans and the sale of munitions to belligerents in any future conflict. The aim was to keep the United States aloof from the political and military strife of Europe and Asia, notwithstanding the ideological complexion of the new totalitarian regimes in Germany and Russia.

The Roosevelt administration was not overly concerned with developments in the Soviet Union. American diplomats and military attachés in Moscow reported on the purges, the industrialization, and the rearmament. They saw Soviet actions as primarily defensive, faced as the Kremlin was with formidable threats from a fascist Germany and an expansionist Japan. Russian arms production and the Soviet military establishment were growing quickly, but report after report from U.S. observers in Moscow noted that the equipment was shoddy, the transportation network inadequate, the technology backward, and the fuel reserves scarce. Military analysts looked with disbelief on the purge of experienced military officers. Stalin, U.S. diplomats agreed, had become a brutal totalitarian leader, but he seemed preoccupied more with safeguarding his regime and his own rule than with expanding Bolshevism abroad.

The real threat to U.S. national security did not emanate from Moscow; it came from Berlin and Tokyo. In 1937, the Japanese resumed their aggression in China. In 1938 and 1939, Germany marched into Austria, seized parts of Czechoslovakia, and eyed the Polish corridor. Roosevelt's attention gravitated to foreign affairs. A steep recession within the larger contours of the Great Depression discouraged him and convinced many of his aides that domestic programs alone could not rejuvenate the economy. The president and his advisors came to believe that the nation's strategic and economic well-being required a revision of the neutrality laws that impeded cooperation with the industrial democracies of Western Europe and with China.

But the circumstances that impelled Roosevelt to look abroad affected other Americans in different ways. A vigorous opposition to the New Deal emerged in 1937–38, and it would remain important for many years to come. The opposition was composed of midwestern Republicans, southern Democrats, conservative businessmen, and determined isolationists. They feared the growing power of the executive branch of the government. Southerners detested the administration's attempts to tamper with racial segregation. Republicans disliked the proliferation of regulatory agencies, the expansion of social-welfare programs, and the attempts to pack the Supreme Court with justices sympathetic to the New Deal. Businessmen resented Roosevelt's calling them economic royalists and abhorred his support for industrial unions. Isolationists of all political persuasions believed the administration's efforts to aid Britain and France short of war might embroil the United States in controversies unrelated to its vital interests and thereby augment the president's powers over the economy and society.

Roosevelt's opponents increasingly suspected that federal agencies were infested with Communists. Support from the Communist Party of the United States of America made the Roosevelt administration especially vulnerable to Red-baiting. Once again, it was the specter of Communism at home rather than the power of Russian Bolshevism abroad that fueled anti-Communist rhetoric. During the 1936 presidential campaign, the Hearst newspapers declared that Roosevelt was "the unofficial candidate of the Comintern," and the Republican vice presidential candidate charged that the administration was "leading us towards Moscow." Antiunion businessmen, fundamentalist Protestants, the Ku Klux Klan, the American Legion, parts of the Roman Catholic hierarchy, and a variety of anti-Semitic groups now jumped on the bandwagon. Businessmen, for example, fought organized labor by alleging that it was inspired by Communism. *Join the CIO and Help Build a Soviet America* was the name of a pamphlet circulated by the National Association of Manufacturers. In 1938 the House of Representatives created a special committee, the House Un-American Activities Committee (HUAC), and placed it under Martin Dies, a veteran Texas Democrat well known for his antilabor stance. The Dies Committee voiced few concerns about Soviet actions abroad, but it worried about Communist penetration of New Deal agencies at home.[26]

Knowing that the Dies committee had considerable public support, Roosevelt moved cautiously. He did not want to outlaw the Communist Party. But he was concerned about disloyalty, about so-called fifth columnists who betrayed their country. After the German and Soviet foreign ministers signed their infamous Non-Aggression Pact in August 1939, the president authorized the use of wiretaps against anyone suspected of subversive activity. He also approved the opening of letters addressed to the diplomatic establishments of the Axis powers.

Roosevelt, however, was still not afraid of Russian power or Soviet goals. Despite the Nazi-Soviet pact, he carefully differentiated between the two countries. When Hitler invaded Poland on September 1, 1939 and started World War II, Roosevelt saw

Germany as the incomparably greater threat to national security. He did not change his mind when Soviet troops marched into eastern Poland at the end of September. Nor did he sever relations with Moscow when the Soviets attacked Finland in 1939 and seized Estonia, Latvia, and Lithuania in early 1940. In the spring of 1941, when Roosevelt asked Congress for lend-lease legislation to assist nations resisting aggression, he inserted language permitting aid to any country. Like most Americans at the time, Roosevelt despised Communism, but he saw Stalin acting in self-defense.

Roosevelt may have been right. One of the most publicized acts of the glasnost years of the late 1980s was the Russians' acknowledgment of the August 1939 secret protocol dividing east-central Europe between the Soviet Union and Germany. But commentators have largely ignored the accompanying documents suggesting that Stalin and his new foreign minister, V. M. Molotov, opted for the Nazi-Soviet pact at the last moment and quite grudgingly. The Kremlin had sought assistance and guarantees from the West. Roosevelt disappointed Stalin by not taking action against Japan and by not selling warships to the Soviet navy. The French and the British agitated Stalin even more by appeasing the Germans at Munich and, in Stalin's view, inviting the Nazis to march eastward. "We would have preferred an agreement with the so-called democratic countries," Stalin conceded to his closest associates, and "we entered negotiations with them, but Britain and France wanted us to be their hired hand . . . and without pay."[27]

The Kremlin lost hope that it could reach a successful accord with the British and the French just at the time that the Germans began pressing for a pact with uncommon haste. Surprised by the German overtures, the Russians initially held back. "Until recently," Molotov told them in July 1939, they "did nothing but curse the USSR."[28] But once Hitler made it clear that he was willing to give Moscow a respite from attack, a defensive perimeter, and a chunk of Poland, Stalin seized the opportunity.

In the fall of 1939, as Britain and France went to war against Germany to stop Nazi aggression, Americans did not know of

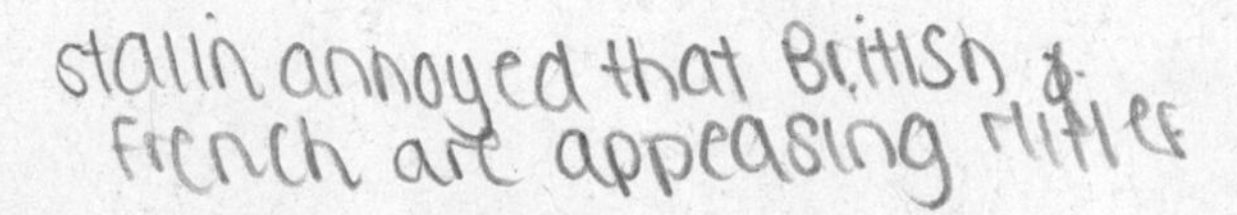

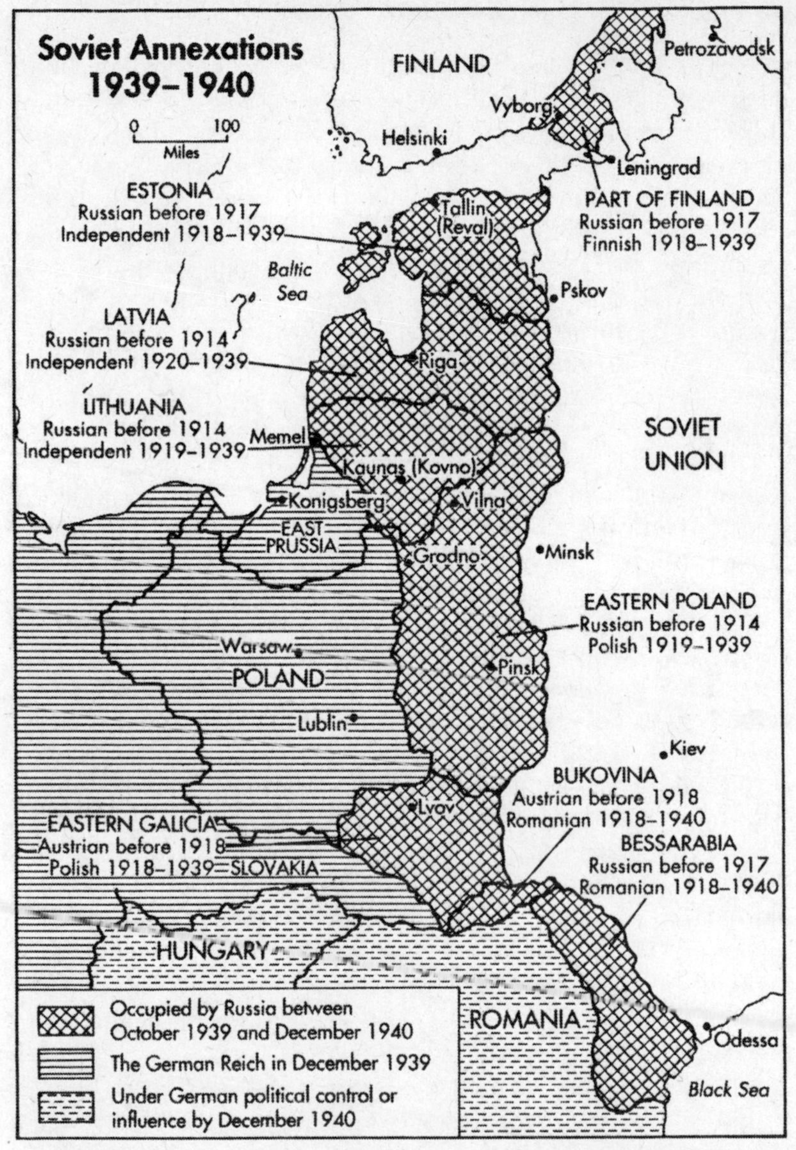

3. Soviet Annexations, 1939–1940

Adapted by William L. Nelson from *Stalin: A Time for Judgement* by Jonathan Lewis and Phillip Whitehead (New York: Pantheon, 1990)

the secret protocol between Hitler and Stalin. But they quickly observed a change in the Kremlin's behavior and in Comintern policy. In 1940, the Soviet Union annexed Estonia, Latvia, and Lithuania and seized strategic territory in Finland. Worse yet, Stalin began selling raw materials to the Nazis and, in 1941, entered into a nonaggression pact with Japan. He also instructed Communist parties abroad to end their popular-front alliances with antifascist parties. Following orders, the American Communist Party turned against the Roosevelt administration's efforts to provide limited aid to France and Britain.

Anti-Communism in the United States surged. Communists could not be trusted, because they had become accomplices of German and Japanese aggression. When Germany crushed Norway, Holland, Belgium, and France in the spring of 1940, many Americans suspected that traitors played a key role. Congress passed the Smith Act, making it illegal for any American to belong to an organization seeking to overthrow the American government. At the same time, twenty-one states passed legislation requiring loyalty oaths from teachers, two states tried to ban the Communist Party from the ballot, and several state governments began to search for Communists within their own bureaucracies.

Although anti-Communism assumed intense proportions in 1940, most Americans still did not dread the power of the Soviet Union. Ascribing Soviet actions to security rather than to ideology, Americans feared not Stalin's Russia but Germany's domination of most of Europe and Japan's quest for supremacy in Asia. The magnitude of the threat was underscored in September 1940 when Germany, Japan, and Italy formed the Axis alliance and signed the Tripartite Pact, evidently aimed at the United States.

Axis power grew formidable. From occupied Europe, Germany gained the resources for unprecedented military-industrial strength. From France and Belgium, the Nazis acquired iron ore, railway equipment, and industrial machinery; from Poland, coal, zinc, timber, and meat; from Romania, petroleum; from Hungary, bauxite; and from Yugoslavia, cop-

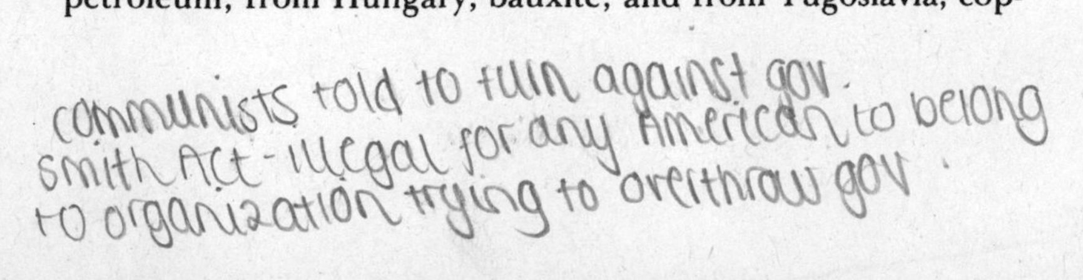

per and chrome. Domination of Europe meant that Germany could also exercise great leverage over key countries in Latin America, like Argentina and Brazil, which sold their grain, meat, and raw materials to the Old World. During 1940, Germany seemed on the brink of vanquishing Britain, penetrating Latin America, and integrating the raw materials and granaries of the Near East, Eastern Europe, and North Africa with the industrial infrastructure, technological know-how, and skilled labor of northwestern Europe. Japan's control of north China and Manchuria, its move into Indochina, and its demands on the Dutch East Indies portended a similar danger in Asia.

The threat was worse than the one that existed in 1918 when Germany had imposed the Treaty of Brest-Litovsk on Russia. "The ghost . . . of a German-Russian domination substantially dominant from the Maginot Line to the Pacific, is becoming more of a reality than I would like to think about," jotted Assistant Secretary of State Adolf Berle in his diary on March 3, 1940. But in 1940, unlike in 1918, the United States was not at war with Germany. Indeed there was a real possibility that Britain and France could capitulate and that an uneasy peace would ensue. "The possibility of a defeat of the Franco-British alliance," Berle lamented on March 23, "must now be squarely reckoned with."[29]

Could the United States live in a world in which the Axis powers dominated much of Europe and Asia? This question triggered a passionate debate during 1940 and 1941 between isolationists and internationalists. Policymakers, congressmen, economists, international-relations experts, businessmen, and newspaper commentators fiercely disputed whether the national security of the United States demanded aid to the Allies in amounts and in ways that might directly embroil the United States in the war.

The position of the Roosevelt administration was clear. The United States, said President Roosevelt in 1940, cannot live "as a lone island in a world dominated by the philosophy of force."[30] Should the Axis nations triumph and consolidate their hold over Europe and Asia, the United States would have to rearm and prepare for an attack. It would have to reconfigure its economy. The government would have to take over the private export sector in order to parry the strength of the government-controlled cartels that the Germans and the Japanese were establishing in their respective areas of domination. Elaborate studies undertaken jointly by the State Department and the Council on Foreign Relations in New York demonstrated that the American political economy—the economy of liberal capitalism—could not survive in a world divided into economic blocs dominated by totalitarian governments.

Yet isolationists feared that Roosevelt would use a war to augment executive power, crush dissent, and transform the American political economy. If the United States goes to war, wrote James D. Mooney in the *Saturday Evening Post,* "we shall pay an appalling price, not only in the lives of our young men and in our food and housing and clothing, but in our precious liberty. . . . On the day war is declared, we can kiss democracy good-by."[31]

But the isolationists had no chance of winning the debate, because most people came to fear that, if the United States stayed aloof from the situation, it would develop precisely those characteristics that the isolationists themselves dreaded. In other words, even if the United States remained at peace in a world dominated by totalitarian foes, it would have to relinquish its basic political and economic values. "If Hitler destroys freedom everywhere else," *Fortune* magazine reported, "it will perish here. Ringed around by a world hostile to our way of life, we should be forced to become a great military power. We should find ourselves dominated and virtually owned by our government—a people in slavery to the state. Industry and trade, labor and agriculture would become part of a state system, which, in its own defense, would have to take on the character of Hitler's system."[32] Mark Sullivan, the well-known commentator, said much the same in January 1941: "Our danger, as it is seen by many thoughtful and competent persons, is the destruction of our American system without invasion."[33] Perhaps nobody put the issue more succinctly than Walter Lippmann, the most renowned journalist of the era, when he wrote: "The fact is that a free economy, such as Americans have known, cannot survive in a world that is elsewhere under a regime of military socialism."[34]

In the view of American internationalists, national security demanded that the Axis be defeated. Strategically, German domination of Europe and Japanese domination of Asia meant that these adversaries might be able to use the resources and labor under their control to attack and wage a protracted war against the United States. But the ideological threat could not be divorced from the strategic menace, because the geopolitical configuration of power meant that Axis domination of Eurasia would force the United States to alter its domestic political economy and to jettison the political and economic freedoms that made it the unique country it was. Neither the progressive individualism of Herbert Hoover nor the welfare capitalism of Franklin D. Roosevelt could survive in a world dominated by Hitler's Germany and Hideki Tōjō's Japan.

In this context it is easy to understand why the United States decided to support Russia when Hitler repudiated the Nazi-Soviet pact and attacked Soviet territory in June 1941. Stalin's Russia was repressive and repugnant; but its strategic and geopolitical interests overlapped with those of the United States. If the Russians could persevere, Roosevelt wrote on June 26, 1941, "it [would] mean the liberation of Europe from Nazi domination—and at the same time I do not think we need to fear any possibility of Russian domination."[35]

Alone, the Soviet Union posed no threat to the United States. But if its resources were assimilated into Hitler's war machine, Nazi strength might become overwhelming. On the other hand, if Stalin's armies could withstand the German onslaught, they might wear down German capabilities and make American intervention in the war unnecessary—or at least reduce the losses and sacrifices that the United States would have to endure. At a meeting in Washington on June 23, 1941, Chief of Staff George C. Marshall expressed his belief that Soviet armies would retreat, destroy their oil facilities in the Caucasus, and deny them to the Germans. But Roosevelt was more hopeful that the Russians could resist, and when signs of this emerged in the late summer of 1941 he was eager to extend assistance to the Kremlin.

Ideological antipathy persisted, but common strategic and geopolitical interests brought the United States and the Soviet Union together. In 1941, Roosevelt and Stalin saw the survival of their systems and their way of life, as well as their territorial integrity, dependent on the defeat of the Axis powers in general and of Nazi Germany in particular. For the Americans the situation was not unlike 1918, when the Germans seemed on the threshold of grabbing Russian resources and turning them against the Western democracies. This time, however, the Bolsheviks had little choice but to fight the Germans, and so American democratic capitalists found themselves allied with Lenin's heirs.

The Japanese attack on Pearl Harbor in December 1941, followed by Hitler's declaration of war on the United States, triggered the alliance between Washington, Moscow, and London. Roosevelt had been slow to aid the British and the French throughout the 1930s, but he demonstrated vision in seeing that common interests now linked the United States and the Soviet Union. So long as there was no sense of threat emanating from Soviet strategic capabilities, American officials could overcome the ideological divide and strike up a working relationship with the Kremlin.

sense of USSR taking the brunt of war

1941- Roosevelt lends resources to Russia
→ US & USSR common strategic & geopolitical interests
- survival: own systems, way life & territory.

(2)

FROM ALLIES TO ADVERSARIES, 1941–1947

THE Nazi attack on June 22, 1941 traumatized Stalin. The dictator who thought he could outmaneuver Hitler was himself outwitted. For months Stalin knew that an attack was coming. He accelerated the rearmament effort and expanded the army. But he did not think that Hitler would invade before the British were defeated. Stalin ignored warnings from his own intelligence agencies and from Western diplomats. One German soldier, a Communist sympathizer, sneaked across the lines just before the attack and revealed the precise moment of the invasion. Stalin would not believe it. He ordered the conscript shot.

Stalin was humiliated by his own miscalculation. German armies advanced toward Leningrad, Moscow, and the Black Sea. They encircled and pulverized Soviet troops. Within a few months, they were on the outskirts of Leningrad, near the suburbs of Moscow, and in control of Kiev and much of the Ukraine. Half the grain crops of Soviet Russia were in German hands, as were 40 percent of the railroads. Three-quarters of a million Russian troops were lost before the end of 1941; almost four million were taken prisoner.

For approximately ten days after the German attack, writes General Dimitri Volkogonov, the preeminent Russian biographer of the Soviet dictator, "Stalin was so depressed and shaken that he refused to be a leader." He was rarely seen; when he was, he was sullen, frail, and full of recriminations. "Lenin left us a great inheritance," he blurted on one occasion, "and we, his heirs, have fucked it all up!" In October, he was on the verge of abandoning Moscow: his goods were packed, a train was waiting, and his family was ready for departure. His country, Stalin realized, might be defeated and his own regime toppled. Secretly, he and Molotov talked about surrendering territory and matériel—a new Brest-Litovsk—if the Germans would cease their fighting.[1]

But Stalin overcame his depression and rallied his people. The war, he now said, was a great patriotic war. The invader had to be repulsed, the fatherland defended. He ceased talking about revolutionary upheaval and cast ideology aside. This was not hard for Stalin, because he had long insisted that the international movement's overriding priority was to safeguard the interests of Soviet Russia. Believing in pure realpolitik, he had been willing to cooperate with the British and the French in the mid-1930s and subsequently with the Nazis, even willing to hand German and Austrian Communists over to Hitler in order to win his goodwill. Ideology served primarily as a lens through which Stalin interpreted threats and opportunities; revolutionary fervor rarely motivated his foreign policy.

When American and British emissaries arrived in Moscow during the summer and fall of 1941, they found Stalin recovered from his depression and indecision. He told them what types of assistance he needed for the protracted war he now envisioned. Even more than aid, Stalin said, he required a second front in Western Europe to divert the Nazi war machine and lift the pressure on his armies.

Stalin's ambitions loomed large when he unequivocally stated that the war must end with the restoration of the 1941 boundaries of the Soviet Union. He would not relinquish the gains he had achieved as a result of the Nazi-Soviet pact of 1939 and the territorial annexations of 1940–41. He wanted the Baltic states, part of Finland, Bessarabia, Bukovina, and the eastern third of pre-World War II Poland.

The second front and the definition of boundaries would be the issues most frequently discussed at the great wartime meetings. But these matters always remained linked in Stalin's mind

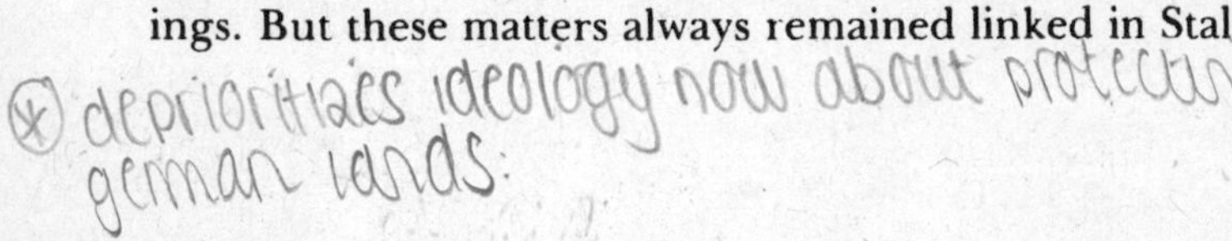

to still more important concerns: the defeat of Germany and the postwar control of German power. As the war dragged on, the toll inflicted by the Nazi invaders became staggering: 8.5 million Soviet soldiers died in action; 2.5 million died of wounds; 5.8 million were taken prisoner, of whom 3.5 million died in captivity. Another 10 million citizens of the Soviet Union perished from starvation or were killed on the home front, many in Stalin's own death camps for alleged treason and disloyalty. The Germans destroyed 1,700 cities and towns and more than 70,000 villages and hamlets. They demolished more than 31,000 factories. They ravaged the agricultural base of the country, ruining tens of thousands of collective farms and slaughtering 17 million head of cattle, 20 million hogs, 27 million sheep and goats, and 7 million horses.

In Stalin's view, Germany was the great enemy—not only a perennial menace to his country but a threat to his regime. After the battle of Stalingrad at the end of 1942, it seemed likely that Germany would be vanquished. But in Stalin's mind, Germany would rise again, just as it had after World War I. In November 1943, at the Teheran Conference, Stalin said he wanted to occupy, disarm, and dismember Germany, liquidate its officer corps, and force it to pay reparations. Even after the war, Stalin believed the Germans would "recover . . . very quickly. Give them twelve to fifteen years and they'll be on their feet again."[2] Throughout the late 1940s, he thought a new war would come and that Germany would instigate it.

Stalin was also deeply concerned about Japan. Japan had intervened against the Bolsheviks during World War I and had been the last of the Allies to evacuate Soviet territory. During the late 1930s, Japanese and Soviet troops skirmished along the Manchurian border and fought several major battles. Stalin sought to neutralize the Japanese by signing a nonaggression pact in 1941. At the Yalta Conference in February 1945 he promised Roosevelt that he would declare war on Japan within three months after the end of the European conflict. In August his armies attacked, took over much of Manchuria, and occupied northern Korea. Roosevelt had said that, in exchange for engaging and defeating Japanese troops on the mainland, the Soviet Union could regain the Kuriles and Sakhalin as well as a dominant position on the Manchurian railroads and in Dairen and Port Arthur. But Stalin still viewed the Japanese with apprehension and did not think they would be ruined even if they accepted unconditional surrender. In July 1945, he told Nationalist Chinese Foreign Minister T. V. Soong that he wanted an alliance in order "to curb Japan."[3]

At the end of World War II Stalin realized that the achievement of his goals—territorial gains, national reconstruction, and control over the revival of German and Japanese power—depended on cooperation with the Allies, especially with the United States. He was inclined to be agreeable because in the short run he was operating from a position of weakness, and he was altogether aware of it.

Stalin had a great deal to gain from a policy of cooperation. Postwar aid would expedite Soviet economic rehabilitation. Even if he was not able to secure loans, he might still extract large reparations from Germany. Most of all, mutual collaboration would mean that he could share in the control of German and Japanese power. At the end of the war, Germany was divided into four occupation zones. Although the Kremlin had a large zone in the east, the core of Germany's potential power—its coal, steel, metallurgy, and chemical industries—was in the western zones, especially in the Ruhr. Stalin wanted to share in some form of international control of the Ruhr. He also sought a real stake in the occupation of Japan.

Of course, Stalin's desire for cooperation had to be balanced against his other goals. He would not compromise his basic territorial demands, that is, the restoration of the 1941 borders. Nor would he forsake a sphere of influence in Eastern Europe. In this region, governments amenable to the Kremlin's influence were vitally important to Stalin. As Soviet troops marched through Eastern Europe in 1944–45, relentlessly pushing Nazi armies back into Germany, Stalin insisted on setting up "friendly" governments.

When the Americans and the British remonstrated against

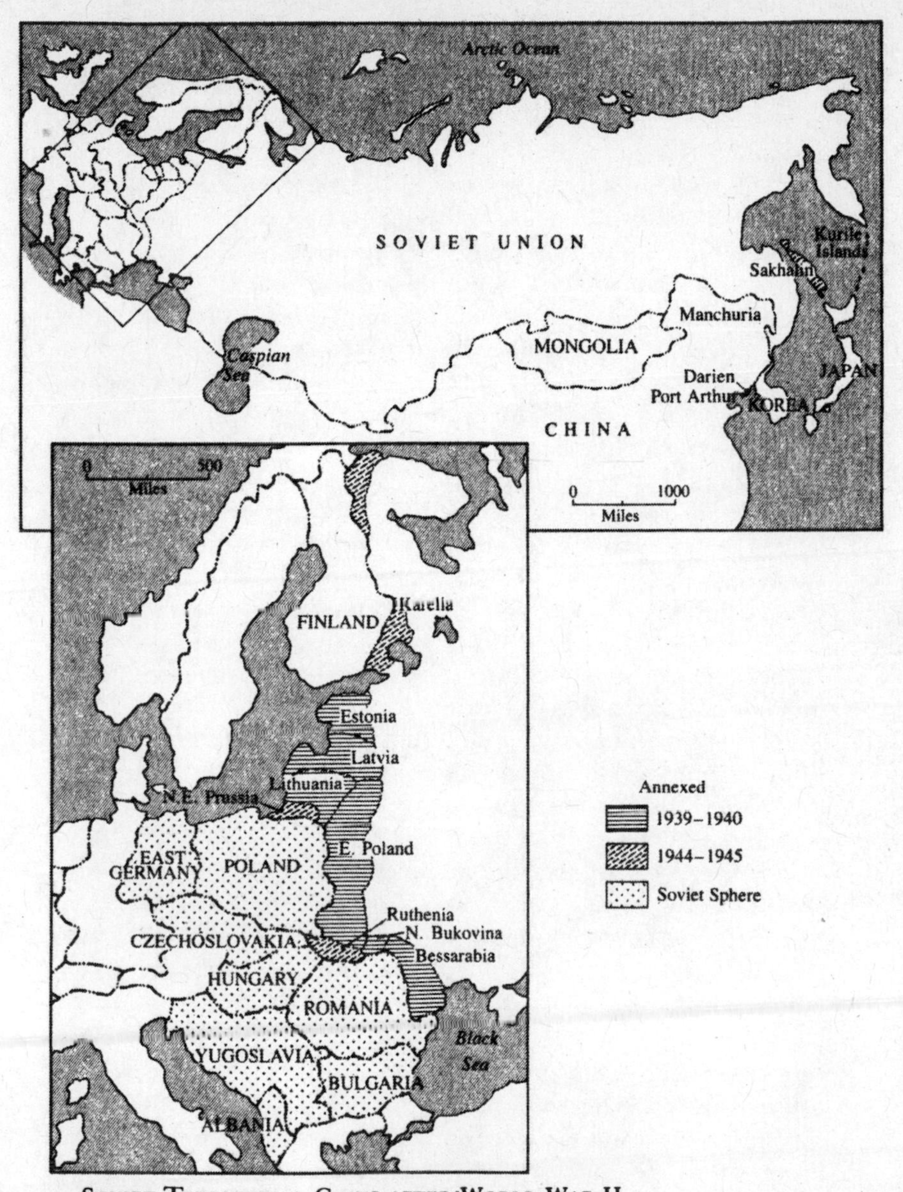

4. Soviet Territorial Gains after World War II

Adapted from *Russia: A History of the Soviet Period*, by Woodford McClellan (Englewood Cliffs, N.J.: Prentice-Hall, 1990)

Soviet intervention in Romania and bitterly protested the Kremlin's creation of a Communist government in Poland, Stalin explained that he had no choice. German armies had marched through Poland into Russia twice in his own lifetime. Before the war, Poland, Romania, and Finland had refused to accede to the Kremlin's security requirements. During the war, Hungary and Romania fought alongside Nazi Germany, and Bulgaria cooperated with Hitler's military commanders. Soviet security requirements mandated a sphere of influence in Eastern Europe. It would serve as a buffer zone against future invasions, a means to facilitate and control the evolution of German power, and a source of raw materials and reparations for reconstruction.

But Stalin's precise plans for Eastern Europe and eastern Germany in 1945 were unformed. As soon as the war was over, he began demobilizing his armies. He withdrew his troops from Bornholm (Denmark) and northern Norway and then from Czechoslovakia. He allowed relatively free elections in Hungary, Czechoslovakia, and Berlin during late 1945 and 1946, and he cooperated in the establishment of representative governments in Finland and Austria. The Soviets seized reparations from eastern Germany and instituted major industrial and agrarian reforms, but they did not lay coherent plans either to communize their own zone or to take over all of Germany. Most of the new evidence emanating from the recently opened archives in Moscow and especially from the archives of Eastern Europe demonstrates that Soviet policies were confused and contradictory, that different bureaucracies in Moscow had different goals, that links between the Kremlin and Communists abroad were intermittent and inconsistent, and that Communists in other countries had some autonomy (if only because Kremlin officials were more concerned with events at home than abroad).

Stalin's approach to international affairs at the end of the war was relatively cautious. He wanted a sphere of influence in Eastern Europe and control of German and Japanese power, but at the same time he wished to sustain the wartime alliance upon which Soviet security and reconstruction depended. To the great dismay of the Communists in France, Italy, Spain, and

Greece, Stalin discouraged revolutionary action in 1944 and 1945, just when they felt their prominent role in wartime resistance movements and their people's genuine desire for thoroughgoing reforms afforded them a unique opportunity to gain power.

Stalin knew that Communist seizures of power would provoke the British and the Americans. To the extent that he communicated with Communists abroad, he insisted that they behave prudently, cooperate with democratic groups, and form coalition or "new type" governments. He urged the new Communist government in Yugoslavia, under Josip Broz Tito, to limit its demands for territory and to stop fomenting insurrectionary action in Greece. He told the Hungarian Communists to restrain themselves lest precipitous action anger the Allies and undercut his efforts to control postwar Poland, the country of greatest importance to Soviet security and one in which resistance to Communist domination persisted until 1947. Stalin's caution, ambivalence, and realpolitik were also evident in China, where he wavered between support for Mao Zedong and the Communists, whom he disdained, and an alliance with Chiang Kai-shek and the Nationalists, whom he regarded with contempt but whose friendship he sought in order to curb Japan and to limit U.S. influence on his Asian periphery.

Safeguarding his periphery was critical to Stalin. Peace was desirable in the short run, because his country had been devastated; but war was likely in the long run, so the Soviet Union needed to be prepared for every eventuality. Stalin knew that one of his country's great vulnerabilities was in the south. From this direction, American and British military planners were configuring an attack should war erupt. Stalin wanted to control traffic through the Turkish straits into the Black Sea, and he sought naval bases, air-transit rights, and petroleum concessions from the governments of Turkey and Iran. But he pursued these goals tentatively, because again they had to be balanced against the goal of maintaining the alliance.

Stalin had to consider whether his allies wanted to preserve the coalition and, if so, whether on terms compatible with his own minimum security requirements. In his view, the atomic monopoly boosted American self-confidence and made the United States more determined to seek cooperation on its own terms. At the Potsdam Conference in July 1945, when President Harry S Truman intimated the existence of a powerful new weapon, Stalin already sensed that the United States was hardening its position. "They want to force us," Stalin told his associates, "to accept their plans on questions affecting Europe and the world. Well, that's not going to happen."[4]

The atomic bombing of Hiroshima and Nagasaki put the Kremlin on the defensive. The situation, recollected Nikita Khrushchev, "weighed heavily on Stalin. He understood that he had to be careful not to be dragged into a war."[5] Stalin ordered the acceleration of Soviet efforts to develop atomic weapons and placed them in the hands of Lavrenty Beria, the head of the secret police. But this did not mean that Stalin discarded his desire to cooperate. The question was whether cooperation could be secured on terms that were compatible with the Kremlin's other goals.

Stalin never laid out a clear approach to any of the problems before him. He was chiefly occupied with safeguarding his own power, his regime, and his country's security and influence. Beyond these fundamental concerns, Stalin's ideas were confused and contradictory. He possessed no distinct strategy on how to pursue his ambitions while retaining Allied support. He acted expediently, zigged and zagged, and uttered pious clichés. Neither his comrades in Moscow nor foreign Communists nor Allied statesmen could discern clear policies, because there weren't any. "To the historian," writes the Norwegian scholar Odd Arne Westad, "Stalin's foreign policy is not as much inexplicable in its parts as incoherent in its whole."[6]

Beneath Stalin, there was an immense amount of internal wrangling going on inside the Kremlin. Stalin was the unchallenged master. "He spoke and we listened," Khrushchev recalled.[7] But in late 1945, Stalin was often silent. Exhausted and ill, he went on vacation. While he recuperated, cunning men and competing bureaucracies struggled to design policies and promote their own interests. We still know too little about what was going on among this second echelon of officials and what advice they were proffering to Stalin. But we do know that the Ministry of Foreign Affairs under Molotov was only one of the key agencies involved in policy-making. The Foreign Policy Department of the Central Committee under the influence of Andrey Zhdanov and Mikhail Suslov, the economic and trade ministries under Georgy Malenkov and Anastas Mikoyan, the secret police under Beria, and the Main Political Administration of the Army under Nikolay Bulganin were all playing a role. For example, there was immense confusion as these different agencies pursued contrary goals in eastern Germany: some were concerned with maintaining order and securing lines of communication; others worried about the seizure of reparations to rehabilitate Russia; yet others were anxious to communize eastern Germany or lure all of Germany into the Soviet sphere.

Inside the Soviet Union there was a renewed emphasis on ideological purification. But the meaning of this for Soviet foreign policy was ambiguous. In his famous election speech of February 1946, for example, Stalin said that the war had arisen as "the inevitable result of the development of world economic and political forces on the basis of monopoly capitalism."[8] This sounded like the resurrection of ideological cant, but when the speech was widely interpreted in the West as a challenge, Stalin sought to correct the impression. In carefully orchestrated meetings with Western reporters, he reaffirmed his desire for peaceful coexistence. He was not hinting at a war between Communists and capitalists, he said, but suggesting the inevitability of conflict between the capitalists themselves, especially the British and the Americans. Although Stalin hoped to take advantage of these rivalries, he also wanted to cooperate with his former allies. And precisely how he could do both at the same time he did not know.

Stalin may have believed that in the long run conflict with the West was inevitable. He retained vivid memories of Western intervention in behalf of the Whites during the Civil War; he believed the capitalist democracies had encouraged the Nazis to attack Bolshevik Russia in the mid- and late 1930s; he was embittered by the delay in the second front; he was infuriated by Western denunciations of his efforts to establish "friendly" governments on his periphery; he was equally exasperated by their attempts to limit the postwar flow of reparations from Germany to Russia; and he was agitated by thoughts that Americans would use their atomic monopoly to extract concessions and endanger Soviet security.

But knowing that for the indefinite future he was in a weak position in relation to the United States and realizing that there was something to gain from cooperation with the West, Stalin moved cautiously. In Poland, Romania, and Bulgaria, he continued to help the Communists consolidate their power. Elsewhere, Soviet policy was restrained. Stalin again urged Tito to act prudently in the Balkans. The Kremlin did not give arms to the Greek Communists and offered only limited aid to the Chinese Communists. Under pressure from the West, Stalin withdrew Soviet troops from Manchuria and Iran.

Throughout 1946 and early 1947, Stalin still beckoned for cooperation both through his rhetoric and through many (albeit not all) of his actions. The Soviets negotiated seriously over the German question at the Moscow foreign ministers' conference in the spring of 1947, and they also agreed to resume talks regarding the unification of Korea. New evidence from the archives in Moscow and the former German Democratic Republic (East Germany) also suggests that the Kremlin was thinking about permitting more pluralist politics inside their zone in Germany and of dismissing some of the hard-line administrators who were seeking to sovietize it. And when no agreement was reached at the Moscow conference, Stalin talked privately to George Marshall, the American secretary of state, and reiterated his desire to reach an accord. Stalin also spoke to Ernest Bevin, the British foreign secretary, and tried to allay his fears about Soviet inroads into the Middle East.

Stalin did not want an all-out rift to occur. The Kremlin was surprised and alarmed when the French Communists left the coalition government in Paris in May 1947 and went into opposition. Stalin still desired cooperation with the Allies and wanted Communists abroad to participate in coalition governments with bourgeois parties. "Cooperation between different systems," he said, "is completely possible."[9] But Stalin had always assumed that cooperation would mean the emasculation of German and Japanese power, the preservation of a Soviet sphere of influence in Eastern Europe, and the protection of the Soviet periphery from foreign interlopers. By the middle of 1947, these assumptions were no longer operative, and, to understand why, it is essential to look more closely at British and American policies.

Top officials in London and Washington also wanted to cooperate with the Kremlin, but on terms that comported with their own respective interests. Winston Churchill, Britain's prime minister, was a renowned anti-Bolshevik who had ardently supported intervention during World War I. In 1940, his antipathy to Bolshevism still burned sharply. But his passionate dislike of the Communists was tempered by his realization that the Nazis constituted the gravest menace to Western civilization. When Germany attacked Russia, Churchill quickly understood that the Soviets would be indispensable in the coalition against Hitler.

Throughout the war Churchill wavered in his attitude toward Stalin and the Russians. He appreciated the immense casualties they were suffering and their need for postwar security, yet he delayed the second front and sought to avoid any territorial settlement that would confirm the 1941 borders. He fumed at Stalin's demands yet admired his wartime leadership. Churchill told the British cabinet in August 1942 that he "had formed the highest opinion of his [Stalin's] sagacity."[10] Although Churchill knew that the Soviet Union would emerge from the war with substantial influence and that it was important to work out proper understandings with the Kremlin, other aims sometimes interfered. He wanted to save British lives on the battlefields, preserve the British empire, safeguard lines of communication through the Mediterranean, and balance Soviet power in Europe.

churchill only wanted to cooperate on his own terms with Nazis & he was hard core anti-communist

Like Stalin, Churchill wanted cooperation on his own terms. He was not certain of Stalin's goals. "Trying to maintain good relations," he confided, "is like wooing a crocodile. You do not know whether to tickle it under the chin or to beat it over the head. When it opens its mouth you cannot tell whether it is trying to smile or prepare to eat you up." In October 1944, he went to Moscow and offered Stalin a deal to divide the Balkans between them. "We have talked with an ease, freedom, and beau geste never before attained between our two countries," Churchill wrote his colleagues in London. At the Yalta Conference several months later, Churchill tenaciously argued with Stalin over Poland and Germany. Yet even after conceding the Polish border that Stalin wanted and after agreeing to language that meant indirect Soviet control over Hungary, Romania, Bulgaria, and Poland, Churchill was pleased with Stalin's respect for British interests in Greece and the Mediterranean. The Soviet leader, he told the British cabinet, was behaving well. "Poor Neville Chamberlain believed he could trust Hitler. He was wrong. But I don't think I'm wrong about Stalin."[11]

In Britain, however, many officials distrusted the growth of Soviet power. Seeking to contain Soviet influence in Eastern Europe and the Balkans, they pondered the establishment of a Western bloc. But they also appreciated Russian sacrifices in the war and recognized that the Soviets were entitled to security. Overall, there was ambivalence and inconsistency in London as well as in Moscow, as policymakers struggled to balance numerous objectives. In each capital, the desire to cooperate was weighed against other priorities and considered in the light of a host of imponderables, including uncertainty about the other side's ultimate intentions.

Churchill was voted out of office in July 1945 and was succeeded by Clement Attlee, the leader of the Labour Party. Attlee's foreign secretary, Ernest Bevin, would play a key role in making British foreign policy for the next five years. An influential trade union leader who had fought domestic Communists for decades, Bevin deeply distrusted the Soviet Union. He detested the totalitarian state and abhorred the maneuverings of the prewar Comintern. Yet he wanted to get along with the Russians, not only because he was aware of the magnitude of their wartime losses but also because he realized that good relations would serve British interests. By the time he took over the foreign ministry, he was prepared to accept a Soviet sphere in Eastern Europe, provided the Kremlin demonstrated self-restraint in Germany, the Middle East, and elsewhere. Given Britain's crumbling power and financial distress, Bevin knew that he needed the United States for diplomatic support and a large loan. His aim was to mobilize American power in behalf of his efforts to cooperate with the Soviets and on terms that comported with Britain's needs.

The Americans were willing to work with the British, but, once again, on their own terms and in ways that did not alienate the Russians. During the war, Roosevelt was renowned for his desire to get along with "Uncle Joe." Some contemporaries and some scholars have excoriated Roosevelt for his alleged naïveté, but actually he was shrewd and pragmatic. Roosevelt knew that at the end of the war the Soviet Union would have a commanding presence on the European and Asian continents. If victory over the Axis was to usher in a period of peace and stability, Roosevelt believed, Soviet-American amity would need to be a component of that postwar order.

Roosevelt, however, realized that a harmonious relationship with the Russians had to be balanced against other U.S. goals. While he sought to soothe Stalin's ego and allay his fears, Roosevelt did not share the secret of the atomic bomb with him and labored to preserve the atomic monopoly. Even Roosevelt's concept of the four policemen—in which the United States, the Soviet Union, Great Britain, and China would keep the peace in their respective spheres—was premised on the assumption that his British ally would exert decisive influence in the Middle East and Western Europe and that China would safeguard American interests in Asia. And although Roosevelt understood that the Kremlin's most vital security requirements were at risk in Eastern Europe, he hoped Stalin would satisfy his strategic needs without too blatantly violating democratic forms. How this could be accomplished was unclear to Roosevelt, because he knew free elections in countries like Poland would lead to anti-Russian and anti-Communist governments. Juggling his concern for self-determination with his desire to preserve the wartime coalition, Roosevelt demanded elections, even if they might be rigged.

Had Roosevelt lived, he surely would have tried to maintain his balancing act. But he died in April 1945, just as the European war was ending and as American and British scientists were racing to complete the atomic bomb so that it could be used against Japan. Vice President Harry S Truman assumed the presidency. He was untutored in foreign policy and military affairs and extremely dependent on the top echelon of officials in the State, War, and Navy departments. Truman asked James F. Byrnes to be his secretary of state and initially relied heavily on his judgment. Byrnes was a former senator, supreme court justice, and overlord of the wartime economy. But Truman also sought advice from Averell Harriman, the U.S. ambassador to the Soviet Union; Admiral William Leahy, the president's chief military aide; Secretary of War Henry L. Stimson; Secretary of the Navy James Forrestal; and other friends.

Truman spoke harshly to Soviet Foreign Minister Molotov in their first conversation on April 22, 1945. The new president accused the Russians of violating their promise to form a democratic government in Poland. His tough words left a lasting impression. "I am convinced," Ambassador Andrey Gromyko wrote in his memoir, that Stalin "took a very unfavorable view of Roosevelt's successor, a man who felt and did nothing to hide his hostility to the power which had borne the heaviest sacrifices in the war against the common enemy."[12]

Yet Truman was not eager for a confrontation with the Russians. Like Stalin, Churchill, and Bevin, he wanted cooperation. Peace, he wrote in his diary, "depended on the wholehearted support of Russia, Great Britain, and the United States."[13] But like the other leaders, Truman felt that the cooperation had to be on his own terms. He did not expect to get his way with the Russians one hundred percent of the time, but he felt "we should be able to get eighty-five per cent."[14] His assessment of his bargaining position was based on the view that the United States had great relative power in the form of its economic strength and strategic might. In mid-July 1945, in the midst of the Potsdam Conference, he also learned that the atomic bomb had been successfully tested in the New Mexico desert and would be ready for use against the Japanese. This was his "ace in the hole," which he could use, firstly, to finish off the Japanese and, secondly, to intimidate the Russians, should it prove necessary to do so.[15]

The new president still hoped it wouldn't be necessary. He and his advisors expected to forge a peaceful and prosperous world order on their own terms. Aside from cooperating with the Russians and the British, the Americans championed the principles of self-determination, open and nondiscriminatory trade, arms limitation, and collective security. Some of these principles resonated through the whole of American history; others, like collective security and arms limitation, were seared into the memories of Truman's generation by Woodrow Wilson. Roosevelt enshrined them in the Atlantic Charter, which he convinced Churchill to sign at their meeting in August 1941.

Almost everyone in official Washington believed that the division of the world into competing economic blocs during the 1930s had deepened the depression, contracted trade, exacerbated political animosities, and bred conflict. An open world would glorify the principles of liberal capitalism, provide the markets for America's agricultural and industrial production, and stymie the accretion of strategic power by other nations that might want to merge their neighbors' resources with their own, thereby gaining local hegemony and preparing the way for additional aggression. In other words, the principles of the Atlantic Charter were not simply abstract ideals but goals desired by the United States because they were thought to comport with American interests, which were also deemed consonant with the interests of world peace and prosperity.

Because self-determination and open trade were supposed to constrain the aggrandizing tendencies of nations, they were closely linked to U.S. geopolitical objectives. The overriding national security goal of the United States after World War II was to ensure that no potential adversary or coalition of adversaries gained preponderant control over the resources of Europe and Asia. When the Japanese and the Germans had gained such preponderance, they attacked the United States and waged protracted war. Even the specter of such a situation would force the United States to prepare for conflict, to reconfigure its economy, to limit political freedoms, and to become a garrison state.

If the other great powers accepted American goals, the United States was eager to get along with them. During the latter part of 1945, American Treasury officials negotiated a $3.75 billion loan to the British in return for their promises to end imperial preferences and to accept an open world based on the convertibility of currencies and nondiscriminatory trade. Truman and many of his advisors were also eager to cooperate with the Soviet Union, provided that the Russians would permit representative governments in Eastern Europe and stop negotiating bilateral trade agreements that tied their neighbors' economies to their own.

Truman was ready to work with Stalin. U.S. officials were indifferent to the brutality and repression of Stalin's dictatorship at home so long as the Kremlin showed restraint abroad. Truman knew that the regime in Moscow was "a police government pure and simple," but he was willing to ignore its internal nature.[16] "I like Stalin," the president wrote his wife after meeting him at Potsdam. "He is straightforward. Knows what he wants and will compromise when he can't get it."[17]

These were not simply the views of a provincial and naïve American politician, as many scholars have claimed. To the contrary, many American and British officials, for all the diversity of their backgrounds, felt essentially the same way as Truman did. "The image of Stalin in our politicians' minds," wrote Frank Roberts, the retired British diplomat, "was increasingly that of this rather quiet, soft-spoken little man who was master of his briefs, seemed to know everything and was not throwing his weight about."[18] Leahy, Byrnes, Marshall, Dwight D. Eisenhower, and Churchill, men of disparate training and experience, shared these sentiments. If "it were possible to see [Stalin] more frequently," Harriman wrote, "many of our difficulties would be overcome."[19]

The men who made U.S. policy were anything but idealists. They cared little about human rights and personal freedoms inside the Soviet Union and the Soviet orbit. They were concerned with configurations of power in the international system and how these configurations affected U.S. interests abroad and, more important, the American political economy at home. Although Stalin, the indomitable leader of wartime Russia, had killed millions of his own people and had authorized the slaughter of thousands of Polish officers at a forest near Katyn, American officials were ready to work with him so long as he seemed respectful of their priorities. At the Potsdam Conference, in fact, the Americans and the British relinquished to the Soviet dictator Russian prisoners of war who had been captured by the Nazis. Stalin quickly transported them to the Gulag, because he trusted no one who had been held in captivity or had been exposed to the West.

For U.S. policymakers, the problem in the aftermath of World War II was not so much Stalin's diplomatic behavior, which was contradictory and ambivalent, as an international system that appeared beyond the control of any government. "There is complete economic, social and political collapse going on in Central Europe, the extent of which is unparalleled in history," reported Assistant Secretary of War John J. McCloy in April 1945. The situation in the Mediterranean was just as grave. "Anarchy may result from the present economic distress and political unrest," Undersecretary of State Joseph Grew wrote the president in June 1945. In Asia, the defeat of Japan bred new strife, reigniting the civil war in China and invigorating national independence movements in Southeast Asia. Summing up the situation in early 1946, Undersecretary of State Dean Acheson told a Senate Committee: "The commercial and financial situation of the world is worse than any of us thought a year ago it would be. Destruction is more complete, hunger more acute, exhaustion more widespread than anyone then realized. What might have become passed off as prophecies have become stark facts."[20]

The Soviet Union was not responsible for these circumstances; the conditions were the legacy of fifteen years of depression, war, and genocide. Nevertheless, with the Kremlin now ensconced in a powerful position in Eastern Europe and northeast Asia, with its regime legitimized by victory in the war, and with Communist parties at the height of their popularity, there was the overwhelming fear in U.S. policy-making circles that the Soviet leadership could capitalize on these systemic conditions. Official Washington was convinced that Communist parties around the world were under the control of Moscow and that if they were to gain power, by means fair or foul, great strategic and economic advantages would accrue to the Kremlin. Truman's advisors were even more worried about the situation in the western zones of Germany. The failure to revive coal production in the Ruhr was retarding recovery throughout the continent, fostering political chaos, and threatening the Communist engulfment of Western Europe. And if the Chinese Communists were to consolidate their hold over Manchuria and north China, American officials believed, the resources of this area would be forfeited to a Soviet superstate.

Truman and his advisors wanted to get along with the Soviets, but they felt they could not permit the accretion of Soviet power beyond the areas already occupied by Soviet troops. Already in 1945, officials in Washington began practicing containment, although it was by no means a comprehensive and well-conceived strategy. In other words, a pattern of actions developed that amounted to containment even before the policy was conceived as such.

The pattern can be discerned by looking at a few examples of U.S. actions in Europe, the Middle East, and Asia. With regard to Germany, the United States and Great Britain rebuffed Soviet desires to participate in the international control of the Ruhr. Secretary of State Byrnes, Secretary of War Stimson, and their expert advisors believed that the resources of this region had to be harnessed to serve the needs of Western Europe and western Germany. Byrnes negotiated an agreement at the Potsdam Conference that limited the reparations the Soviet Union could receive from outside its own zone. Russia, said one of the president's briefing books, had already been left "as the sole great power on the Continent—a position unique in modern history."[21] Nothing should be done that might further enhance that power.

The State Department and the Joint Chiefs of Staff also decided in July 1945 that Soviet overtures for base rights in the Turkish straits must be rejected. From the Dardanelles, the Soviets might envelop additional areas of Asia Minor, jeopardize British control of the Mediterranean, and achieve a dominant position on the Eurasian landmass. The United States, said American war planners, could not take such chances. "Russia might be sorely tempted to combine her strength with her ideology to expand her influence over the earth."[22]

The Truman administration likewise sought to limit the growth of Soviet influence in Asia. The United States occupied southern Korea and denied the Kremlin any influence in postwar Japan. Truman and his advisors sent marines to China, where they initially assisted the Nationalists in their struggle against the Communists while helping to repatriate Japanese troops back to the home islands. And in Southeast Asia, American lend-lease supplies and naval convoys facilitated the return of the British, the French, and the Dutch to their former colonies.

These limited actions were designed to stop the accretion of Soviet and Communist power even while Truman and his colleagues were convinced that they still wanted to get along with the Kremlin. These steps were taken at a time when the president was also anxious to satisfy popular demands to bring American boys home from the battlefields of Europe and Asia, to convert the economy to peacetime purposes, and to scale down spending and reduce taxes. With these considerations in mind, the administration quickly demobilized American armies, released research scientists and weapons experts from national service, and reduced relief and rehabilitation assistance.

At the end of 1945 there was no coherent strategy, but there were immense fears in policy-making circles about the future configuration of power and its meaning for liberal capitalism at home and abroad. Soviet actions were mixed, but the potential threat loomed large. Truman and his aides increasingly riveted their attention on the Kremlin's ominous conduct and overlooked signs of Soviet moderation. They discounted the demobilization of Russia's own armies, the free elections in Hungary and Czechoslovakia, and the establishment of representative governments in Finland and Austria. They also minimized the Kremlin's willingness to cooperate in Germany, its deference to the U.S. position in Japan, its readiness to accept an American presence in southern Korea, and its restraint in aiding the Chinese Communists. Instead, Truman and his aides denounced Soviet intervention in Bulgaria, Romania, and Poland; they rebuffed Soviet requests for bases in the Turkish straits; they ridiculed the Kremlin's seizure of factories in Manchuria; and they warned Moscow to stop intruding in the politics of northern Iran and to pull Russian troops out of that country. At the end of the year Truman was convinced that the United States had to "stop babying the Soviets." He mused, "Unless Russia is faced with an iron fist and strong language, another war is in the making."[23]

The president was predisposed to a tough policy even before the State Department received George F. Kennan's long telegram from Moscow in February 1946. This message from the highest-ranking foreign-service officer in the Soviet Union remains one of the landmark documents of the early Cold War years. Soviet leaders, Kennan wrote, were motivated by traditional Russian insecurities and Marxist-Leninist dogma. They used the specter of capitalist encirclement and foreign hostility to justify their totalitarian rule at home. They wanted to expand everywhere and take advantage of every opportunity. Portraying Soviet fears as irrational and misrepresenting Stalin's own rhetoric, Kennan said the United States could do nothing to mollify the men in the Kremlin. He urged his superiors in Washington to overcome their ambivalence, identify the Kremlin as the enemy, and approach all issues from the perspective of competition with the Soviet Union.

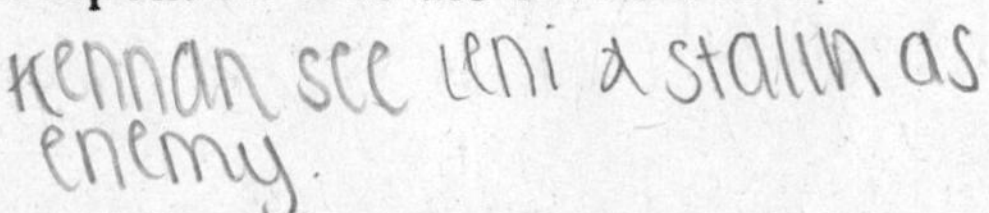

Several weeks later Winston Churchill visited the United States. After reviewing his address with aides to the president, the former British prime minister, with Truman sitting by his side, made it clear that he had resolved any ambivalence he formerly possessed. "From Stettin in the Baltic to Trieste in the Adriatic," Churchill told his audience at Westminster College in Fulton, Missouri, "an iron curtain has descended across the continent." Beyond the curtain, Communist parties endangered Western civilization. Going further than Kennan, Churchill called for an Anglo-American alliance and for joint strategic planning.[24]

Truman and his advisors were by no means willing to go that far themselves. But Churchill's eloquent warning and Kennan's blunt analysis helped resolve any lingering ambivalence. Changing perceptions of the Kremlin relieved officials of the need to try to reconcile their diverse geopolitical and economic goals abroad with their desire to get along with the Kremlin. Policymakers need not agonize over the problems of accommodating legitimate Soviet interests; the Soviets had none. Policymakers need not scrutinize avenues for compromise; it was futile. Having identified the Kremlin as a totalitarian foe akin to Nazi Germany, they could adopt a strategy designed to thwart the growth of Soviet power in peacetime or to defeat it in wartime.

The fact that most officials in the Truman administration wanted to go on the offensive was made abundantly clear during the summer of 1946. Two of the president's closest aides, Clark Clifford and George Elsey, consulted with virtually every high-ranking member of the administration and wrote a report that reverberated with the language of Kennan and Churchill. The Kremlin, they emphasized, was seeking "to weaken the position and to destroy the prestige of the United States in Europe, Asia, and South America." The United States had to "assist all democratic countries which are in any way menaced or endangered by the U.S.S.R."[25]

Truman agreed with this analysis but was not yet ready to take action. After reading the Clifford/Elsey report, he ordered that all copies be locked up in a White House vault. He himself carefully avoided public rhetoric that revealed his personal animus toward the Soviet Union. He did not think the American people were ready to bear the costs and incur the commitments that went with a policy of containment. He also knew that the progressive wing of his own party, led by Secretary of Commerce Henry Wallace, was not ready to admit the impossibility of continued amity with the Soviet Union.

Truman bowed to pressures from hard-line advisors to fire Wallace, but publicly he refrained from using inflammatory rhetoric. Bold action on the eve of the 1946 congressional elections might backfire politically, because the administration, in Clifford's words, was "far ahead of the American public" in wanting to take the initiative.[26] The Republicans were assailing Truman for not ending the wave of postwar strikes and for failing to curb inflation and lower taxes. An admission that postwar harmony with the Soviet Union was now impossible would fuel Republican charges that the administration had been inept, that it was soft on Communism, and that its failed efforts would now mean higher taxes and higher prices.

The 1946 elections, therefore, were fought over domestic issues. "Had enough?" the Republicans asked the American electorate. The voters resoundingly said yes. The Democrats went down to a humiliating defeat. The New Deal coalition, tottering since 1938, was now smashed. For the first time since 1928, Republicans gained control of both houses of Congress. Truman's stature plummeted to an all-time low; chances for his reelection appeared hopeless.

Right after the elections, Truman confided to his staff that he felt a new sense of freedom. Since he had nothing more to lose, he now wanted to act boldly in pursuit of the policies that he and his advisors had already deemed necessary. Fearful that Republicans would cut military expenditures, reduce aid, and provide inadequate funds for the occupations of Germany, Japan, Korea, and Austria, Truman was willing to assert his leadership. If he did nothing, the international situation would likely crumble and Republican recriminations would grow. Naming George Marshall his new secretary of state was an omen. Marshall had been chief of staff of the army during

World War II and had become one of the most revered men in the nation. Upon taking over the State Department, he assured Republicans that he sought no partisan advantage and he beckoned for their cooperation.

The need for action seemed more imperative than ever during the winter and spring of 1947. Everywhere around the globe vulnerabilities grew and avenues for Soviet gains developed. In China, the civil war intensified. Chiang Kai-shek's position deteriorated largely because he thought he could defeat the Communists militarily and because he was unwilling to make concessions and undertake reforms. In Southeast Asia, the French and the Dutch became locked in military struggles with revolutionary nationalist movements that demanded immediate independence. In the Middle East, the British were unable to work out a satisfactory deal with the Egyptians over their rights to the great air base at Cairo-Suez. Experiencing no more success ironing out differences between the Zionists and the Arabs, the British planned to withdraw from Palestine.

If those political developments were not worrisome enough, the economic situation in Western Europe made tensions worse. The winter of 1947 was harsh, the snows heavy, and the temperatures frigid. There was insufficient food and fuel. Western European governments struggled to save their precious dollars, entered into barter agreements with one another, and tried desperately to sustain their recovery. But they implored the United States for more food, coal, and dollars. Unless help was received, middle-of-the-road politicians in France and Italy warned, the local Communists, partners in the existing coalition governments, would exploit the situation, gain votes, and take power. In a typical message to Washington, the American ambassador in Italy reported that "all the indications we receive . . . show that the Communists are consistently gaining ground."[27] Conditions in the occupied zones of western Germany were no better. Major food riots erupted, prompting General Lucius Clay, the U.S. military governor, to remonstrate "over the rapid penetration of communism."[28]

More ominous still was the financial bankruptcy threatening

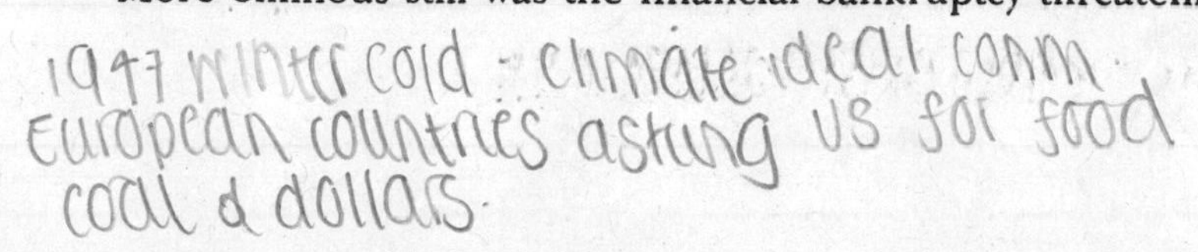

England. The government was quickly using up the American loan and running out of dollars. Attlee and Bevin realized they had to cut back; they could not achieve their reforms at home while maintaining their traditional policies abroad. In February, they told the Americans they were going to pull out of Greece and suspend their assistance to Turkey. They wanted Washington to assume the burdens of containing Soviet expansion.

This was a decisive moment in the origins of the Cold War. In March 1947, the president announced the Truman Doctrine and offered a package of military aid and economic assistance to Greece and Turkey. At the same time, Truman and his advisors decided that, to relieve the burden on American taxpayers and to provide France and other Western European countries with sufficient coal, they had to boost Germany's level of industrial production. And in order to win the loyalty of the German people themselves, American officials resolved to support the unification of the three western zones and the formation of a new German government. These actions were accompanied by the most famous initiative of all, the Marshall Plan—not so much a plan as a promise to extend large amounts of aid to European countries that demonstrated a willingness to tighten their belts and coordinate their recovery plans.

The inducements to take action once again had little to do with Soviet behavior. U.S. officials certainly did not believe that the Kremlin was contemplating unprovoked and premeditated military aggression. Soviet actions had not become more threatening, but the international situation had worsened and the Soviet Union could capitalize on systemic weaknesses. The crisis in Greece, for example, had become more portentous not because of Stalin's aid to the Greek Communists but because of Britain's decision to withdraw. Nonetheless, if the Greek Communists gained the upper hand in the civil war, American officials thought, it would have a bandwagon or domino effect elsewhere. If the United States did nothing, Truman recalled in his memoirs, its "lack of interest would lead to the growth of domestic Communist parties in such European countries as France and Italy, where they already were significant threats.

Inaction . . . could result in handing to the Russians vast areas of the globe now denied to them."[29]

Even if the Russians were restrained, the situation would remain harrowing. Everywhere in Europe governments were resorting to exchange controls, barter agreements, and national planning in order to husband scarce resources and even scarcer dollars. Truman and his advisors were terribly fearful of the implications of all this. In a major speech on foreign policy at Baylor University on March 6, 1947, the president lamented the growing impediments to international trade and vividly discussed the interrelationships between political and economic freedoms. Free enterprise in the rest of the world, he said, was jeopardized by the devastation wrought by the war and by the requirements of reconstruction. Nations felt compelled to regiment their economies and practice autarky, or self-sufficiency. Much of the world was heading toward central planning, and the meaning of this for the American people was grave. The United States would increasingly have to adopt new measures to fight for markets and raw materials. It would have "to find itself in the business of allocating foreign goods among importers and foreign markets among exporters and telling every trader what he could buy or sell, and how much, and when, and where. . . . It is not the American way. It is not the way to peace."[30]

Domestic political and economic systems could not remain insulated from patterns of international trade and from configurations of power in the international system. U.S. officials were convinced that regimented trade abroad, bilateral barter agreements, and state planning would eventually jeopardize economic and political freedom at home. "The deterioration of the European economy," wrote the president's Committee on European Recovery, "would force European countries to resort to trade by government monopoly—not for economic but for political ends. The United States would almost inevitably have to follow suit. The resulting system of state controls, at first relating to foreign trade, would soon have to be extended into the domestic economy to an extent that would endanger the survival of the American system of free enterprise."[31]

The configuration of power in the international system was the thread connecting foreign economic distress and the prospective decay of liberal capitalism at home. Communist parties would feel most comfortable with domestic regimes that set priorities, regimented trade, and controlled financial transactions. They would look to Moscow and sign bilateral trade agreements with the Kremlin, as had already happened in Eastern Europe. The Soviets would respond eagerly, seeing such mechanisms as levers to spread their influence and gain control of additional resources. According to the president's advisors, dominoes would fall and the ramifications for the United States would be dire: "If the countries of middle-western and Mediterranean Europe sink under the burden of despair and become Communist, Scandinavia will fall into the same camp. The strategically and economically vital North African and Middle Eastern areas will follow. This transfer of Western Europe, the second greatest industrial area in the world, and of the essential regions which must inevitably follow such a lead, would radically change the American position. If it should prove that a weakened United Kingdom could not resist so powerful a current, the shift would be cataclysmic."[32]

The way to mobilize the American people to support vast new commitments and expenditures abroad was to convince them that their basic freedoms were at stake. Republicans were reluctant to go along, and so, too, were many Democrats. Truman's foreign policy advisors told him that he needed to shock the American people into action. Dean Acheson found that he was most persuasive to Republicans when he warned that inaction exposed all of Eurasia to Soviet penetration. In his speech to the American people announcing the Truman Doctrine, the president said "a fateful hour" had arrived and nations "had to choose between alternate ways of life."[33]

Anti-Communism resonated deeply in the American psyche. Since World War I Bolshevik ideology had been repugnant to the American people. Now that that ideology was linked to the second most powerful nation on the globe, the threat seemed harrowing indeed. As in 1940 there was the prospect that an adversary with a hostile ideology and a totalitarian government might gain control over the preponderant resources of Europe. The adversary was even more insidious because it was likely to achieve its goals without the use of force. It could capitalize on the successes of Communist parties and revolutionary nationalist movements or exploit German disillusionment and Japanese demoralization. These former enemies, Truman and Marshall feared, might be drawn into the Soviet orbit by the lure of Soviet markets or by promises of territorial rectification. Soviet and German power could merge, as had been feared in 1917–18 and in 1940, but this time under Soviet tutelage. Stalin, much like Hitler, was not likely to invade the Western Hemisphere; but by forcing the United States to live in a closed political and economic environment, the Soviet Union could threaten to erode the American way of life. Secretary of Commerce Averell Harriman's advice to Truman in 1947 resonated with the same rhetoric he used in 1940 when he warned, "It would be very difficult, if not impossible, for one democratic state to live in a totalitarian world without modifying materially the country's life."[34]

Republicans and other prospective opponents found it difficult to resist the administration's rhetoric, because anti-Communism resonated deeply with their own ideological predilections, with their constituencies, with their life experiences, and with their political self-preservation. Even while the Soviet-American alliance was in its heyday, religious fundamentalists, segregationists, antiunion businessmen, and patriotic organizations sustained the fight against Communists at home. In California, for example, the Tenney Committee—one of many committees formed in state legislatures to investigate "un-American activities"—bitterly attacked the labor movement, saying that it was infiltrated with Communists. The Tenney Committee won support from businessmen in war-related industries, such as electronics, airplane construction, and base maintenance, and from newspaper publishers, like the Hearsts and the Chandlers, who sought to crush the remnants of the New Deal. This anti-Communism appealed to a new generation of Republican politicians, including Richard Nixon, whose own congressional district south of Los Angeles was part of Jack Tenney's constituency. In many such districts in California, Texas, and the South, the connections between anti-Communist politicians of both parties and union-busting farm and business groups were close.

In these areas, moreover, religious ultraconservatives often joined with right-wing extremists and racial segregationists. They equated the struggle against Communism with the eternal battle between Satan and Christ and with the quest to preserve a white-dominated regime in the South. Truman's anti-Communist rhetoric played well. How could local politicians assail Communists at home and not be concerned with their power abroad? Truman locked many Republicans and southern Democrats into supporting an internationalist foreign policy, notwithstanding the fact that they cared more about fighting local battles against unions and African Americans.

But anti-Communist rhetoric was powerful also because many liberals and progressives (as well as conservatives) were sincerely troubled by Soviet power abroad and potential subversion at home. The decision of the American Communist Party to support the Nazi-Soviet pact of 1939 made its followers seem like Stalin's puppets and cast a permanent pall over its activities. Inside American unions, leaders like Walter Reuther of the United Automobile Workers waged a ferocious struggle against Communists, claiming that their loyalty was to Moscow rather than to the union and the country. Reuther wanted to purge the Communists because their presence made the entire union vulnerable to outside criticism. He was acting in the perceived self-interest of his union, but his own rhetoric contributed to the anti-Communist fervor gathering in the country.

There was another reason why Truman's message gained a sympathetic hearing. The American people had just finished dealing with one totalitarian threat. Another was now appearing on the horizon. Americans were not eager to incur commitments and extravagant expenditures abroad, but they possessed powerful images linking totalitarianism, repression, and expansion.

Immediately after the war, popular magazines portrayed the Soviet Union ambivalently, both as heroic ally and potential geopolitical threat. It possessed an alien ideology, a dictatorial government, a mighty presence, and a propensity to expand. "Russia," said *Life* magazine in July 1945, "is the number one problem for Americans because it is the only country in the world with the dynamic power to challenge our own conceptions of truth, justice, and the good life."[35] Initially, most Americans were uncertain whether the Kremlin would pose such a threat. But as news spread of Soviet repression in Poland and Romania, of delayed withdrawals of troops from Manchuria and Iran, and of the power of Communist parties in France, Italy, and Greece, fears multiplied. In the popular news media, like *Time* and *Newsweek*, and in mass circulation magazines, like *Life* and *Look*, stories of Stalinist repression, Soviet totalitarianism, Communist agitation, and Soviet expansionism proliferated. These accounts rekindled memories of Axis aggression and fifth-column insurrectionary activity. Columnists and journalists, of course, were increasingly fed these stories by their contacts within the administration. But the images they conveyed and the associations they engendered ensured a favorable reception to Truman's announcement that the world was split into competing ways of life.

The administration shaped public opinion, but it was not purely manipulative. The president and his advisors felt real apprehension. They feared not a Soviet attack but the growth of autarky and state planning, the strength of Communist parties, the vacuums of power in Japan and Germany, and the vitality of revolutionary nationalist movements. The Kremlin could capitalize on all these developments. If nothing was done, George Kennan warned his superiors, the United States would face a Europe that "would be no less hostile to us" than the Europe "of Hitler's dreams." Every foreign service officer he knew, Kennan continued, believed "that the dimensions of the deterioration would be great enough to require not only a major and costly readjustment of our political-military strategy but also changes in our domestic life."[36]

Realists like Kennan did not compartmentalize foreign and domestic affairs; they were keenly aware of how configurations of power shaped the domestic political economy. Nor were these ideas unfamiliar to politicians of all stripes and to the attentive public. "If western Europe," said William Knowland, California's Republican senator, "goes behind the iron curtain . . . the whole productive potential of that section of the world will fall into the Russian orbit . . . [and] the repercussions upon our own domestic economy would be . . . terrific."[37] And in a similar vein, the editors of the *Saturday Evening Post* wrote that the United States had "to reconstitute civilized life and decent political and economic relations in the world, if we want those conditions to continue here at home."[38]

This larger sense that a whole political economy of freedom was at stake shaped the U.S. diplomatic offensive in 1947. Policymakers sought to contain the Soviet Union because they felt that correlations of power in the international system had a significant bearing on political freedoms and a market economy at home. These factors were much more important than prosaic economic considerations, like the anticipated slump in exports if European economic and financial conditions worsened. Some officials stressed the economic dimension, but most shared the view of the Council of Economic Advisers: "It is a mistake to suppose that we are dependent upon the current size of the export surplus to preserve our prosperity."[39] But hardly anyone thought it was a mistake to believe that autarky, state planning, and further Communist gains in Europe would compel "sweeping" alterations in "our economic and political life."[40] It might mean, warned Assistant Secretary of State Will Clayton, "basic change in our Constitution and Bill of Rights."[41]

By the middle of 1947, most Americans were inclined to view the struggle with the Soviet Union as an ideological one between contrasting ways of life. This was an apt characterization because American policymakers saw themselves waging a geopolitical battle over correlations of power in the international system, a battle whose reverberations carried enormous implications for the political economy at home. Changing power relationships,

Truman's advisors told him, "would force us to adopt drastic domestic measures and would require great and burdensome sacrifices on the part of our citizens."[42] If under worst-case scenarios the United States was compelled to protect itself against a totalitarian foe with a command economy and a resource base covering much of Eurasia, the American government might have to regiment its own economy, hike defense spending, monitor potential subversives, and curtail personal liberties. The United States, Truman acknowledged, might "have to become a garrison state" with "a system of centralized regimentation unlike anything we have ever known."[43]

With America's political economy of freedom seemingly at risk because of portentous changes in the global balance of power, it is no wonder that the Truman administration moved decisively to an adversarial relationship. The foreign policy challenge, as Dean Acheson liked to stress, was "to foster an environment in which our national life and individual freedom can survive and prosper."[44]

(3)

ASSUMING HEGEMONY, 1947–1950

THE Truman Doctrine, the Marshall Plan, and the initiatives in Germany were decisive moves in the development of the Cold War. They arose as a result of fear—fear that vacuums of power, financial hardship, exchange controls, popular Communist parties, and revolutionary nationalist movements might play into the hands of the Soviet Union. So long as Communism was primarily a hostile ideology, it was reviled and contested at home; when it was linked to a totalitarian adversary with great military potential and with the capacity to capitalize upon systemic weaknesses and economic dislocation, it had to be contested abroad. Gradually, between 1947 and 1950, the United States took on the role of hegemon in the international system and in so doing accepted responsibility for revitalizing the international economy, thwarting the spread of Communism, and guaranteeing the security of its partners.

American initiatives, in turn, triggered great fears in the Kremlin. Until the middle of 1947, Stalin contemplated cooperative arrangements with the West and tolerated a semblance of pluralism and private enterprise in countries like Czechoslovakia and Hungary. All this changed after June 1947. Perceiving threats to its security, the Kremlin tightened its grip on its satellites; seeing new signs of Soviet aggression and repression, the U.S. moved with alacrity to organize the rest of the world. The "security dilemma" came into operation as each side moved to enhance its security, thereby provoking additional fears in the adversary and producing new countermeasures that tended yet again to intensify apprehensions and underscore vulnerabilities.

Since all European countries were theoretically invited to participate in the Marshall Plan (or the European Recovery Program, as it was sometimes called), the Kremlin had to decide how to respond to the American initiative. Nikolay Novikov, the Soviet ambassador to the United States, reported to Moscow that the Marshall Plan was an effort to inject American power onto Russia's periphery. Contending that the Truman Doctrine had not aroused much support in Britain and France, Novikov believed that the offer to extend economic aid was yet another device "to bring European countries under the economic and political control of American capital." He and Deputy Foreign Minister Andrey Vyshinsky warned Molotov that the United States was trying to forge an anti-Soviet bloc in Western Europe, deny Russia reparations from Germany, and erode Soviet influence in Eastern Europe.[1]

Yet the Soviets desperately needed aid, and they could not simply ignore the invitation from the French and the British to join them in Paris for an assessment of the American offer. Molotov went to the French capital in early July 1947 with a large contingent of advisors. He wanted to ascertain whether Russia and its satellites could get aid without having to sacrifice their sovereignty and economic independence.

After spending a few days in Paris talking to the British and French foreign ministers, Molotov had his answer. "Under the guise of formulating a plan for the reconstruction of Europe," he informed Stalin, Western statesmen were seeking "to establish a Western bloc with the participation of western Germany." The Americans, Molotov concluded, were trying "to interfere in the internal affairs of European countries, impose an American programme upon them, and ban them from selling their surpluses where they choose to, thus making the economies of these countries dependent on US interests."[2]

Yet Stalin and Molotov knew that their Eastern European comrades were tempted to take whatever risks were necessary in order to obtain American credits and expedite their own reconstruction. Stalin himself was uncertain about how to handle the situation. But after a few days of indecision, he resolved that the governments within his orbit must not participate in the Marshall Plan. "Using the pretext of credits," Stalin told a Czech delegation, "the Great Powers are attempting to form a Western bloc and isolate the Soviet Union."[3]

The evidence from Russian and Eastern European archives now confirms that this was a critical moment in postwar Soviet policy. Stalin saw that the bourgeois parties in France and Italy had squeezed the Communists out of coalition governments. He watched the Americans moving into Greece and establishing a presence on Russia's southern perimeter in Turkey. He observed them trying to co-opt German power, terminate reparation payments to the Soviet Union, establish a Western bloc, and penetrate the Soviet sphere in Eastern Europe. The invitation to the Kremlin and its partners in the East, he judged, was a sham, simply an effort to gain participation on terms that would open them to Western capital and lure their critical raw materials, like Polish coal, westward. In retrospect, writes General Dimitri Volkogonov, it is clear that the Marshall Plan would have expedited Russian reconstruction; but Stalin, he concludes, rightly rejected it because it posed unacceptable threats to Soviet security and might have meant "US control over the Soviet economy."[4]

The Kremlin decided that it had to defeat the Marshall Plan. In September 1947, Stalin convened a meeting of European Communists in Poland and reestablished the Comintern, now called the Cominform. At the meeting, the two Soviet representatives, Georgy Malenkov and Andrey Zhdanov, launched an ideological offensive against the West and condemned the popular-front strategy. The more the war receded, Zhdanov declared, the more evident was the division of the world into two hostile camps. Assailing American imperialism, Zhdanov said that the Marshall Plan was designed to subordinate recipient countries to U.S. economic and political domination. He called upon his fellow comrades to fight the Marshall Plan and to cease collaboration with any groups that supported it.

The fierce attack on the West concealed as much as it revealed, for we now know that Stalin was also striving to gain the unquestioned obeisance of Communist parties in other countries. In particular, Stalin sought to humiliate French and Italian Communists who had participated in postwar coalition governments and who occasionally acted without conferring with Moscow. More important still, he was scheming to outmaneuver Tito, who had been the true apostle of revolutionary action, who had been operating independently in the Balkans, and who had been complaining about Russia's exploitative trade arrangements with Yugoslavia.

Rather than foment insurrection abroad, Stalin's true aim was to get foreign Communist parties to serve the interests of the Soviet state more effectively. He wanted them to fight the Marshall Plan, assist reconstruction in Russia, and align their foreign policy with his own. Faced with the prospect of a revived Germany and a Western bloc, Stalin now demanded rigid compliance and total subordination. French and Italian Communist leaders launched a series of strikes and demonstrations. Workers walked out of factories; ex-partisans went on parade; violence flared. At the same time, Stalin's minions in Hungary and Czechoslovakia denounced the Marshall Plan, plotted against their opponents, and maneuvered to gain a monopoly of power.

American officials were not surprised by the Soviet response. On November 6, 1947, Secretary of State Marshall told his cabinet colleagues that he expected the Kremlin to clamp down on Czechoslovakia. George Kennan and Charles Bohlen, the two ablest Kremlinologists in the State Department, agreed. In their view, Soviet actions were a "quite logical" reaction to U.S. initiatives.[5] The American intent was not to threaten the Soviets or divide Europe, but this was the price the Truman administration was willing to pay in order to revitalize Western Europe and harness the resources of western Germany.

Yet in the months following the announcement of the Marshall Plan, conditions did not improve. The drought in Western Europe worsened, food supplies disappeared, German coal production stagnated, and Britain experienced a terrible gold drain. Western European diplomats met to discuss their requirements for financial aid under the American-led recovery program, but the exaggerated figures they generated and the nationalistic plans they prepared left their American counterparts frustrated. Meanwhile, the Communist insurgency in Greece grew, and the prospects for a Communist victory in Italy in the spring 1948 elections mounted. The situation, Kennan wrote, "was deteriorating with terrifying rapidity."[6]

In France, Italy, and Greece, local Communists seemed on the verge of winning or seizing power. Should they do so, American officials believed, they would negotiate bilateral treaties with the Kremlin similar to those already signed by the USSR and its Eastern European satellites. The Kremlin would bind the economies of these nations to Soviet Russia and at the same time gain special base privileges. Slowly and irrevocably Soviet strength would grow while American capabilities would decline. Secretary of Defense James Forrestal warned that if Europe, with all its industrial and military potential, were integrated "into a coalition of totalitarian states, it is possible that we in time would find ourselves isolated in a hostile world."[7] The United States would then have to reconfigure its domestic political economy and augment its military expenditures. A totalitarian Europe, Truman's advisors told him at the end of September 1947, would mean that "a great part of what we have fought for and accomplished in the past would have been lost. . . . The sacrifices would not be simply material. With a totalitarian Europe which would have no regard for individual freedom, our spiritual loss would be incalculable."[8]

The Truman administration sought to convince Congress and the American people that the crisis was grave. This was no easy task, because the Senate and the House of Representatives were dominated by Republicans who were scornful of foreign aid and desirous of lowering taxes, slowing inflation, curbing the powers of the executive branch, repudiating the New Deal legislative program, and winning the White House in the 1948 presidential election. These Republicans were not at all interested in dishing out dollars to Europeans, and they despised the idea of enlarging the powers of the State Department. They preferred to embarrass the administration, alleging that it was riddled with traitors and soft on Communism.

In November 1947, Truman called a special session of Congress. Acknowledging that the Marshall Plan would not be ready until early 1948, the president asked legislators to approve an emergency aid bill. Secretary of State Marshall, Secretary of Defense Forrestal, and Secretary of Commerce Harriman warned Congress that unless $600 million was immediately granted to France, Italy, and Austria, these countries would gravitate into the Soviet orbit. If the Republicans refused support, they would be accountable for endangering the nation's security and allowing the Reds to take over Europe. As one hesitant Republican congressman acknowledged: "We get it from all sides by official speakers, the press and the radio. They all say the same thing—either vote for this aid to Europe or all Europe will go communist."[9]

The strategy sought to lock the Republicans into support for an American leadership role around the world. Truman's political advisors believed that the special session of Congress and the emergency relief bill boosted the president's political standing. They knew that fighting Communism resonated with the American people as did no other foreign policy slogan, because Communism was seen as an alien ideology poisonous to private enterprise and democratic pluralism and repugnant to ethnic Americans who saw their brethren in Eastern Europe oppressed by the Soviet behemoth. In the minds of Americans, Soviet Communism was now no different than Nazi totalitarianism.

Truman administration officials did not simply exploit popular anti-Communism in demagogic fashion for ulterior purposes. Although Truman and his advisors did not fear a Soviet attack on the United States, they felt as Roosevelt and his aides had in 1940, when the latter were dreadfully worried about the long-term consequences of Nazi domination of Europe. Although in retrospect we can see that the situations were not parallel—the maneuvering of the Soviet Union and the actions of European Communist parties in 1947 were far less bold than Nazi military conquests in 1940—Clark Clifford's advice to Truman resembled Roosevelt's thinking seven years earlier. "The issues involved," Clifford privately wrote Truman, "are of such importance as to take precedence over all other questions, and the consequences of failure are too grave to permit the President to stop anywhere short of the full use of his Constitutional powers in his efforts to meet the requirements of the situation."[10]

The administration, therefore, moved ahead with its attempts to contain Communism, even while Congress debated the interim aid bill. In November 1947, Secretary of the Army Kenneth Royall and Army Chief of Staff Dwight D. Eisenhower recommended that the United States send ninety military advisors to Greece to offer operational advice to the forces fighting the Communist uprising. In the following months, Truman also considered the deployment of U.S. combat troops. At tense meetings of the newly created National Security Council, Secretary of State Marshall ruminated on the commitments inherent in the Truman Doctrine and declared that the country "could not escape the dire consequences" if it did not back up its policies.[11] The president's advisors, tempted to commit troops, held back because they feared the domestic political costs of partial mobilization and because they knew that the same soldiers might be needed elsewhere.

Italy was the place where they might have to go. Although Kennan, now the head of the State Department's Policy Planning Staff, generally discounted the possibility of war with the Soviet Union, he nevertheless thought that U.S. troops might have to be used against the Italian Communists. He encouraged the Joint Chiefs of Staff to expedite contingency plans for direct military intervention. The numbers were small, but the administration did beef up its naval presence in the eastern Mediterranean, sent 1,000 marines to join the Sixth Fleet, and readied a reinforced regimental combat team in Germany for an emergency airlift to Italy.

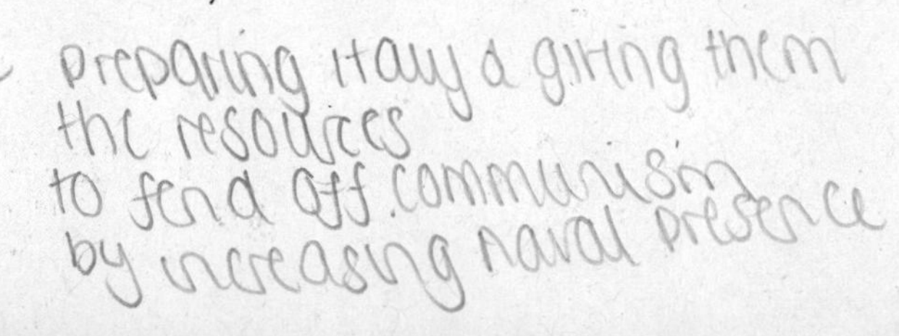

While U.S. policymakers pondered the use of troops to meet immediate contingencies, they preferred to build up local forces of resistance in countries like Italy and France. In order to help the moderate Italian government of Alcide De Gasperi win the forthcoming elections and resist a Communist coup, Secretary of Defense Forrestal and Undersecretary of State Robert Lovett sent military supplies and authorized covert operations against the Italian Communists. At the same time, Secretary of State Marshall approved highly confidential talks with the French, the aim of which was to provide military supplies to the French government so that it would be able to cope with Communist uprisings should they occur. The State Department and the Central Intelligence Agency also used secret funds to intensify the splits brewing in the French and the Italian labor movements. U.S. officials wanted to support moderate socialists in their struggle to form workers' movements independent of Communist domination.

Of far greater long-term significance were the initiatives in the western zones in Germany. During 1946, the British and the American zones had been merged. At the time that Marshall announced his European Recovery Program, the United States also decided to boost the permissible level of industrial production in Germany. American officials were certain that the reconstruction program for Europe could not work unless coal production in the Ruhr was increased and unless German resources and markets were integrated with those of Germany's neighbors in the West. If this did not occur quickly, Marshall and Lovett believed, the whole of Germany might be lured into the Eastern orbit.

American leaders, therefore, looked with great trepidation on the autumn 1947 meeting of the Council of Foreign Ministers. Germany was again the central topic of conversation, and Marshall dreaded the possibility that the Soviets might suddenly seem conciliatory and offer a surprise package calling for the withdrawal of occupation troops, the payment of reparations, and the establishment of a united and neutral Germany. Such an initiative could undermine the Marshall Plan before it began,

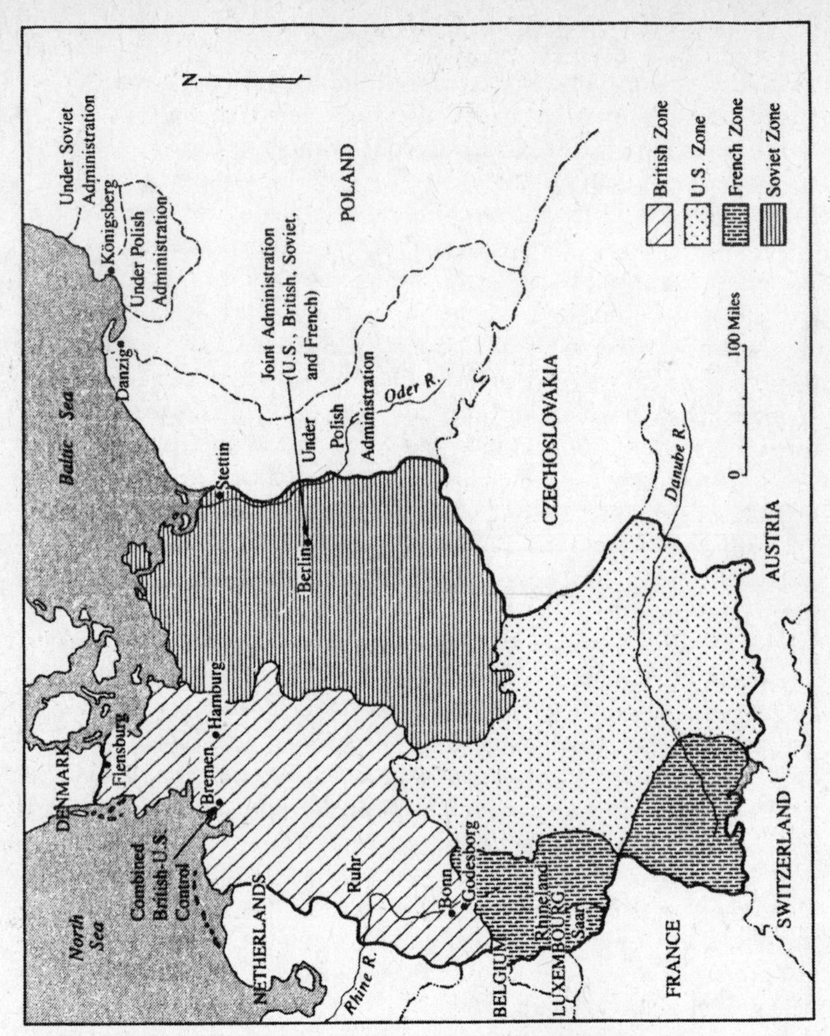

5. Germany after World War II: Occupation Zones

Reprinted from *A Preponderance of Power*, by Melvyn Leffler, with the permission of the publishers, Stanford University Press.

while opening all of Germany to Soviet penetration or Communist subversion.

Before the foreign ministers convened in London, the Americans and the British met secretly and decided to rebuff any Soviet overtures that might deflect progress on the European Recovery Program. When Molotov arrived, he lambasted the Marshall Plan and stridently reiterated Soviet demands for reparations from current production. Mixing his tirades with some concessions, he seemed to be signaling a willingness to engage in tough bargaining if Marshall and Bevin were willing to do so. But they were not, and breathed a sigh of relief when the conference broke up. Their greatest fear, acknowledged one of the American delegates, was that the Kremlin might have proposed a deal adroitly packaged to capture German support yet cleverly designed to prevent German participation in the European Recovery Program. The Germans, Kennan noted at the time, remained "sullen, bitter, unregenerate, and pathologically attached to the chimera of German unity."[12]

In the aftermath of the London conference, General Lucius Clay and Sir Brian Robertson, the American and British military governors in Germany, moved with great haste to boost German morale and German production. They revised the bizonal economic council and established a bizonal central bank. Clay, in particular, pushed for currency reform and German self-government. The Americans desperately wanted to merge the French zone with the other two Allied zones, win over German sentiment, and mobilize German resources for the European Recovery Program, which the administration was then putting before Congress.

The French posed an enormous obstacle. The far right and the far left, now composing almost a majority in French political life, looked with equal horror on Anglo-American initiatives in Germany. Indeed all Frenchmen, even moderates like Premier Robert Schuman and Foreign Minister Georges Bidault, wavered over the wisdom of augmenting German production, restoring German coal mines and steel furnaces to German management, implementing currency reform, and accepting the restoration of German self-government. A revived Germany, even a revived western Germany, might gain considerable autonomous economic and military power or might align with the Kremlin, seeking thereby to achieve reunification with the East and the repossession of territory taken by the Poles (with Soviet support) at the end of the war. "What is worrying French officials," wrote the commander of the American fleet in the Atlantic, "is SECURITY. They are scared of the colossal ground forces to the eastward. They are afraid that, if Germany is resuscitated, her resources and technical proficiency would be used by the U.S.S.R. against France. They want some concrete assurances that . . . in case of attack, they could preserve part of Metropolitan France from invasion and another occupation."[13] In short, the French wanted military aid, staff talks, a commitment to defend the Rhine, extensive international controls over the Ruhr, and guarantees to ensure German demilitarization.

After the meeting of the foreign ministers in December 1947, the British realized that they had to create a Western European bloc that would reassure the French, entangle the Americans, and deter the Soviets. In vague terms Foreign Secretary Bevin outlined his hopes to Marshall before the American secretary of state returned to the United States. Bevin wanted to establish a Western union that at its core would include Britain, France, Belgium, the Netherlands, and Luxembourg. The focus would be on Germany. On January 22, 1948, Bevin presented a blueprint to Parliament. Almost immediately, his European partners agreed to open discussions. Five days later, Bevin invited the United States to discuss a separate bilateral defense arrangement that would buttress the prospective Western union.

During the winter of 1948 two critically important consultations moved forward: one relating to the formation and reconstruction of western Germany, the other pertaining to the defense arrangements required by the re-creation of potential German power. The parallel talks were inextricably intertwined: all the participants understood that the discussions regarding Germany had the danger in the short run of provoking the Kremlin and in the long run of creating a defiant and uncontrollable Germany. Although Germany was now weak, demoralized, and under the control of the four occupation powers, European and American officials knew they were putting in motion a train of events that might escape their control.

The British and the Americans were acting out of a sense of genuine fear. Should Germany, or at least the western zones, not be integrated into the European Recovery Program, the Marshall Plan would have no chance of succeeding. And if the program failed, European autarky, or self-sufficiency, would grow, indigenous Communists would gain additional support, and the Germans would become increasingly disillusioned with the West. These developments would play into the hands of the Soviet Union, whose ambitions seemed confirmed by their denial of national autonomy to Romania, Poland, and Bulgaria, by their demands on Turkey, by their formation of the Cominform, and by their apparent eagerness to capitalize on Western distress and division.

From Stalin's perspective, the opportunities seemed more questionable and the dangers more formidable. Famine still racked parts of the Soviet Union; guerrilla warfare was just subsiding in the Ukraine, Belorussia, and Lithuania; and the demoralization and despair of the Russian people mounted. Stalin wanted to safeguard his periphery, control German power, and utilize indigenous Communists in Western Europe to enhance Soviet influence and strength. But he saw the United States trying to rebuild and co-opt German power while Britain was forging a new Western alliance. At the same time he was agitated by the efforts of Tito's Yugoslavia to conduct an independent foreign policy in the Balkans. While the Marshall Plan was an open attempt to lure his satellites westward with promises of markets and dollars, the formation of a west German republic with hopes for economic revitalization might also serve as a magnet for his own east Germans. Stalin, then, had to worry about the near-term threat of a west German state coopted into a hostile alliance and a long-term threat of an independent, reconstructed, and reunited Germany reemerging as a dominant power in central Europe.

Faced with crisscrossing sets of opportunities and threats, Stalin protested Western initiatives in Germany and tightened his grip over Eastern Europe and eastern Germany. He negotiated a series of bilateral defense pacts with Germany's former satellites, the aim of which was to restrict their ability to act independently. He also encouraged his minions in Eastern Europe to take their own steps to solidify their control. In Bulgaria, they executed the opposition leader Nikola Petrov; in Poland, they accused seventeen non-Communist leaders of supplying information to the underground and tried them as traitors; in Hungary, they expelled members of the Social Democratic and Smallholders' parties from the government and forced them to flee for their lives. And in Czechoslovakia, the Communists took advantage of a parliamentary crisis to grab legal control of the government. With the Kremlin's support, they proceeded to crush the opposition. Before February 20, 1948, Czechoslovakia was a democratic state, with a Communist plurality, a foreign policy oriented to accommodate Soviet requirements, and an economy still knitted to the West. After March 1, it was a Communist dictatorship, ostensibly a symbol of the fate that awaited any country that accepted Communists into coalition governments.

The American people were stunned by events in Czechoslovakia. They compared the internal coup of 1948 with the Munich crisis of 1938 and the ensuing Nazi military takeover of Czechoslovakia. The press and the media in the United States talked of war.

Truman and his advisors were genuinely worried. They did not fear a premeditated Soviet military attack, but developments in Czechoslovakia underscored the fragility of democratic institutions and the weakness of democratic parties in Europe. In Prague, the non-Communist parties had capitulated. Would the democratic parties in France and Italy also falter? Would the Communist success in Czechoslovakia animate their comrades in other countries to grab power?

For U.S. officials, the Czech crisis underscored the importance of bolstering the morale and determination of democratic forces in Western Europe. Schuman in France and De Gasperi in Italy had to be reassured that, if they sided with the United States, Washington would help protect them against internal unrest and external pressure. Marshall and Forrestal agreed that Western European allies now had to receive military aid and security guarantees. Schuman and De Gasperi had to know that, if they had the political courage to rebuild Germany, control inflation, and defy local Communists, the United States would help to thwart indigenous uprisings, control the resurgence of German power, and deter Soviet counterthrusts. In fact, the United States would soon do something it had never done before: it would negotiate a peacetime military alliance, the North Atlantic Treaty, with its European friends. NATO

Signifying the severity of the situation, Truman appeared before a joint session of Congress on March 17, 1948. He charged the Soviets with violating agreements, destroying the independence of Eastern European governments, and scheming for political gains and strategic advantage in Scandinavia. He implored Congress to pass the European Recovery Program and to enact universal military training and selective service. He declared that the United States had to keep its occupation forces in Germany until the peace in Europe was secure.

That evening, the president gave a St. Patrick's Day address in New York and talked in more ominous terms about international developments. "The issue," he said, was "as old as recorded history. It is tyranny against freedom." Communism denied the very existence of God. "This threat to our liberty and to our faith must be faced by each one of us." To do so required great risks, indeed the greatest risks in the country's history.[14]

During the following weeks the risks and obligations that the president had in mind became clearer. He asked Congress for a $3 billion increment in military spending. The money was to be used for additional military personnel, the procurement of aircraft, the reactivation of bases, and military research and development. At the same time, he authorized top-secret talks with the British and the Canadians about the formation of an

Atlantic alliance that would be linked to the European Western Union. He instructed his subordinates to sound out Arthur Vandenberg, the Republican chairman of the Senate Foreign Relations Committee, about the possibilities of passing a resolution permitting U.S. association with a European regional alliance system.

Truman's quest for a bipartisan foreign policy worked. Republicans remonstrated against the costs, but passed the Marshall Plan. Republicans objected to universal military training, but passed the Selective Service Act. Republicans lambasted the administration for not reducing taxes, but then appropriated even more funds than Truman requested for a military buildup. Republicans attacked the administration for disregarding the importance of China, but then supported the Vandenberg resolution and set the stage for the consummation of the North Atlantic Treaty.

Truman's anti-Communist rhetoric was marvelously effective. His political advisors were convinced that strong leadership and bold talk against the specter of Communism would redound to the president's political advantage and revive his chances for victory in the 1948 elections. Republicans assailed the Democrats for betraying the country's interests at the wartime summit conferences, for coddling pinkos and labor unions, and for spending extravagant sums of money. By underscoring the threat of Communism and linking it to Soviet power, Truman now locked these same opponents into supporting foreign aid, military spending, and strategic commitments.

A Cold War consensus formed. Truman was willing to fight domestic subversives, as the Republicans demanded, in return for their support of his foreign policy. The president instituted a loyalty program requiring all federal employees to pass an investigation by specially created boards in all the departments of the federal government. Attorney General Tom Clark and FBI Director J. Edgar Hoover issued a list of subversive organizations and initiated a campaign to deport aliens who were Communists. Truman's commissioner for education launched a crusade to reassess high school curricula in order to ensure that American youth were adequately prepared to combat Communism.

The administration also collaborated with the House Un-American Activities Committee. In March 1947, at the time he was proclaiming the Truman Doctrine, the president permitted J. Edgar Hoover to testify before HUAC. The FBI director declared that the Communist Party was a fifth column intent on overthrowing the American government. In this way Truman hoped to steal HUAC's thunder and prevent the Republicans from capitalizing politically on the issue of disloyalty. The president sought to convert widespread fear of domestic subversion into support for his foreign-policy initiatives.

When HUAC investigated the film industry in late 1947 and accused screenwriters of Communist affiliations, the Justice Department moved quickly to secure indictments. Alleged Communists were blacklisted, and the motion picture industry promised not to employ anyone threatening to overthrow the American government. Thereafter, the film industry hesitated to make movies with a serious social message and concentrated on war films, escapist fantasies, and anti-Communist pictures. Truman and his advisors did not initiate the campaign against domestic Communists and radicals, but they were willing to use it to boost support for the Marshall Plan and the North Atlantic Treaty.

Politicians and businessmen who were eager to attack radicals, unions, and civil rights advocates found it convenient to tap into the anti-Communist consensus. The aviation industry, for example, had been reeling from the postwar cutbacks in military spending. Industry spokesmen joined with military officials and with senators and congressmen from affected areas to exaggerate the external threat in order to restore company profitability, boost local employment and revenues, and enlarge Air Force capabilities. The 1948 appropriations gave the aviation industry a new lease on life. Likewise, southern segregationists, faced with a new round of civil rights demands, latched on to the discourse over subversion to defend their way of life and to label proponents of integration as Communists. Businessmen also used the rhetoric of anti-Communism to bolster their postwar assault on unions. They inserted provisions into the 1947 Taft-Hartley Act that required union officers to sign anti-Communist affidavits. Even university administrators found ingenious ways to use anti-Communism to serve parochial interests. Communism "is the mortal enemy of everything for which the University of Virginia stands," said its president, Colgate Darden, in late 1947. "Support the development plans of the University of Virginia."[15]

Many participants in the anti-Communist crusade did not have the same goals as Truman and his advisors. But Republicans and southern Democrats who wished to use anti-Communism to fight radicals, unions, and civil rights advocates at home could hardly object to the administration's efforts to fight Soviet power and Communist influence abroad. Against their own desires, many Republicans grudgingly gave assent in 1948 and 1949 to the Marshall Plan, the North Atlantic Treaty, and a military assistance program. They acquiesced in the administration's desires to rebuild German and Japanese power and to maintain U.S. troops in those countries. They even nominated Governor Thomas E. Dewey of New York, an internationalist, to run against Truman in the 1948 election.

Americans from different regions, social strata, and economic backgrounds accepted a new role for the United States, the role of hegemon, in the international system. This meant that the United States gradually assumed responsibility for rebuilding Europe, reviving its former enemies, ensuring the security of its friends, and overseeing the smooth functioning of the world economy. Different groups supported this role for different reasons. Some shared the beliefs of Truman's advisors. If the United States did not take action, they assumed, the Kremlin could gain preponderant power in Eurasia, thereby threatening U.S. security and forcing it to become a garrison state with a governmentally-controlled economy. Others were more concerned with radical changes at home, the power of labor unions, and the growth of federal and executive power. They were willing to accept a hegemonic role for the United States in the international system and a worldwide containment policy only if these steps enhanced, or did not interfere with, their ability to reduce the influence of organized labor, thwart the proponents of racial integration, and boost local economies dependent on military contracts and base development. Senator Kenneth Wherry of Nebraska, for example, was one of the strongest Republican critics of the administration's foreign policy, but he happily accepted the selection of his home state as the headquarters of the Strategic Air Command.

While cultivating domestic constituencies, Truman administration officials also worked diligently to gain foreign acceptance of America's leadership role abroad. They did this primarily through persuasion, inducements, and financial leverage. They did not simply dictate to potential allies. They responded to their needs, often modifying American demands to accommodate the national aspirations of Allied governments and the desires of influential elites within those nations. In fact, the weaknesses of some governments, like those in France and Italy, often turned out to be their strengths. The threat of indigenous Communist gains gave moderate leaders like De Gasperi and Schuman leverage against U.S. desires that they cut their budgets or earmark monies for uses they did not want. Although the United States induced the French through economic aid, security guarantees, and military assistance to accept German rehabilitation and German self-government, Washington nonetheless deferred to France's leadership role in Western Europe, accepted its desire to forge supranational institutions like the European Coal and Steel Community, and helped finance its postwar economic program, the Monnet Plan. Similarly, although the United States convinced Attlee and Bevin to accept the principles of multilateralism and to forgo the socialization of the Ruhr coal mines (under British control in Germany), the Truman administration did not try to reverse the nationalization of British industries or retract Labour's social-welfare programs. Nor did the Americans force the British to integrate themselves into a European customs union.

For U.S. officials and European elites there was a convergence of purpose: to contain indigenous Communism at home and Soviet power abroad. The Communist seizure of power in Czechoslovakia impelled moderate politicians in France and Italy and officials in Washington to work together and to compromise their different agendas. Although this would be a long and tedious process, there were some immediate, heartening results. In Italy, De Gasperi won an overwhelming victory in the April 1948 elections. By accenting the choice between freedom and totalitarianism and by capitalizing on the promise of Marshall Plan monies, De Gasperi's Christian Democrats routed the Communists. And two months later, France's middle-of-the-road government felt so fortified with promises of economic aid and military support that it went to the Chamber of Deputies and secured legislative approval of the program designed to put at least the western parts of Germany on the road to economic renewal and self-government.

Just as the West had been alarmed by the Communist clampdown in Czechoslovakia and by the Kremlin's efforts to negotiate treaties with Finland and Norway, the Soviets now felt beleaguered by Western initiatives in Germany, the security talks over an Atlantic alliance, and the defeat of the Italian Communists. Stalin's response was to blockade Berlin. Soviet troops would not allow trains and trucks to move through their zone in eastern Germany on the way to the former German capital, which at the end of the war had been divided among the allied victors (see map on page 72). The Kremlin made it clear that its intent was to compel the Americans, the British, and the French to reverse their decisions to merge the western zones of Germany, to create a federal republic, and to reform the German currency. Stalin feared the recrudescence of German power and its incorporation into a Western alliance system. Knowing that he was about to break with Tito, Stalin felt that he needed a diplomatic triumph. If he could not get Washington, London, and Paris to reverse their decisions regarding western Germany, he hoped the blockade would force them out of Berlin. Either way he could reap a great victory.

The blockade of Berlin created the greatest crisis of the early

NATO, joining zones, the defeat Italian comm & Tito falling from his grip → contributed to blockade

Cold War. Truman, Marshall, and Forrestal would not back down. Nor would they abandon Berlin. In one way or another they were determined to get supplies through eastern Germany to the western sectors of the former German capital. General Clay wanted armed convoys to roll down the German autobahn. The Russians, he believed, were bluffing and would not try to stop the Americans lest they provoke a war they could not win. Truman, Marshall, and Forrestal agreed that the Russians did not want war. But neither did they, and a convoy that directly challenged the blockade might trigger an incident or engage Soviet prestige in ways that could lead to war through miscalculation.

Truman decided to airlift supplies to the western sectors of Berlin. Some of his defense advisors doubted whether the airlift could succeed over a long period of time and questioned whether the deployment of so many aircraft to Germany dangerously weakened the United States elsewhere. But Truman agreed with Clay that withdrawal from Berlin or repudiation of the accords to create the Federal Republic would demoralize the western Germans, undercut the European Recovery Program, and strengthen the Communist tide everywhere in Europe.

Withdrawal from Berlin would also shatter the president's chances for reelection just as the party conventions were taking place. Truman's political fortunes depended on his gutsy fight against the "do nothing" Republicans at home and the specter of Communism abroad. To back down in Berlin just as he was attacking the Republicans and calling a special session of Congress would be political suicide; the Republicans would have crucified him.

To demonstrate his determination, Truman sent two groups of B-29 bombers to England. Such planes were capable of delivering atomic bombs to their targets inside the Soviet Union. However, the aircraft that were actually deployed were not properly outfitted for an atomic mission. Truman and his aides hoped the Russians would not know this and would be impressed by the show of strength.

Soviet spies in Washington probably alerted the Kremlin to

the truth about the American aircraft. Stalin, however, remained cautious. For a few days in July and again in early September, officials in Washington, London, and Paris worried about the eruption of hostilities, but for the most part everyone was impressed by the fact that the Soviets made no effort to interfere with the airlift of supplies to Berlin.

Soviet circumspection confirmed American assumptions that the Kremlin would probe and pressure and try to exploit favorable conditions but would avoid open conflict. The Russians were weaker than the Americans, and both sides knew it. The United States and its partners in Western Europe could move forward with their daring initiatives to establish a West German government. They would reform its currency, revitalize its economy, and integrate it into the European Recovery Program. Although these measures, as Clay predicted in April 1948, had precipitated "the real crisis," they could not be abandoned.[16]

Diplomatic and economic risks had to be taken. Otherwise, German coal production would falter, the economies of Western Europe would suffer, trade deficits would mount, and exchange controls would grow. European peoples might despair. They would vote for leftists or rightists and accept more government controls and regulations. The Germans themselves would become even more demoralized, succumb to Soviet blandishments or pressures, and gravitate to the East.

To prevent these possibilities, the United States had to take risks. And it had the relative power to do so. Although there were only a few dozen atomic bombs in the U.S. arsenal in 1948, the Soviets had none. Although American conventional strength was meager, its potential war-making capabilities were vast. Should conflict erupt, the Soviets might overrun Western Europe, but they had no capacity to strike the United States. Slowly but surely American strength would grow, its economy would convert to war, its strategic air power would overcome Soviet air defenses, and its atomic capabilities would devastate Soviet cities. When Secretary of State Marshall talked to European diplomats in the fall of 1948, he discreetly alluded to the atomic monopoly as the West's trump card. Atomic weapons were not only critical for warfare; they were indispensable in peacetime, inspiring the confidence to proceed with bold initiatives, such as the European Recovery Program, the North Atlantic Treaty, and the formation of a West German state.

The Kremlin retreated before U.S. demonstrations of strength. Stalin was fearful of war and recognized Soviet weakness. Soviet war plans during the early postwar years were defensive in nature, and Soviet military exercises often practiced strategic retreat. Rather than challenge the airlift, Stalin tried to outmaneuver the West diplomatically. He failed, and in May 1949 he abandoned the blockade.

These were trying and frightening times inside the Kremlin and the Soviet bloc. Stalin's lieutenants schemed against one another. Zhdanov's followers were now outmaneuvered by Malenkov and Beria. The losers disappeared; some were murdered. Foreign Minister Molotov was unexpectedly replaced by Vyshinsky. The meaning of this was unclear at the time and is not fully understood even now.

But other developments were more transparent. Stalin excommunicated Tito from the Cominform and purged potential dissidents within Eastern European Communist parties. Rather than look for new opportunities in Western Europe, the Soviet dictator consolidated his bloc and acquiesced in the defeat of the Greek Communists. Stalin allocated greater resources to his own military establishment and waited eagerly for Soviet scientists to break the U.S. atomic monopoly. Looking for opportunities to recapture the momentum and erode the West's strength, he turned his attention to the civil war in China.

During 1948 and 1949 Chinese Communist forces under the leadership of Mao Zedong routed the Nationalists on the mainland and forced Chiang Kai-shek to establish his government on the island of Taiwan. Stalin viewed this development as one of the great events of the postwar years. Much as he distrusted Mao, he now hoped the Chinese Communist Party (CCP) would serve as the Kremlin's agent in Asia. Stalin was willing to concede considerable autonomy to the Chinese and accept a preeminent role for China in Asia, so long as Mao

chiang = nationalist & develops nationalist gov on Tiawan.

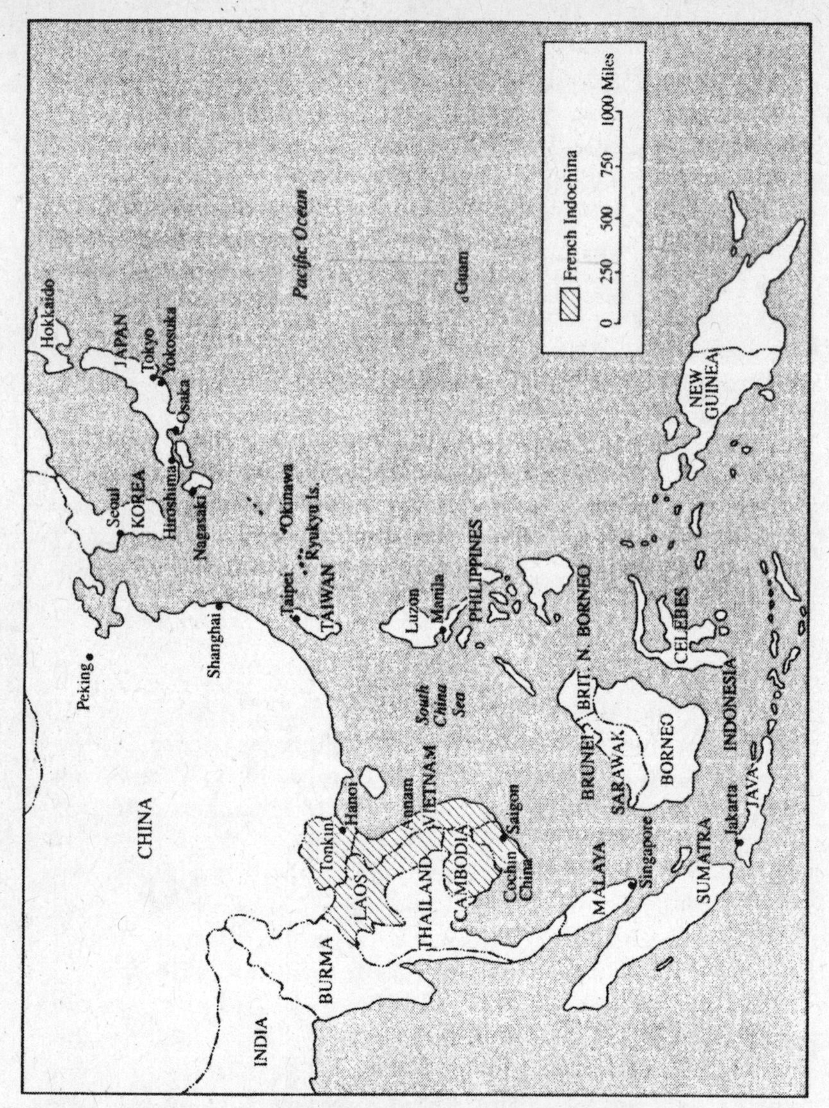

6. East and Southeast Asia: 1948

followed Stalin's lead in his relations with the West and did not challenge Soviet security requirements in northeast Asia.

The Chinese Communist victory stirred deep misgivings in Washington policy-making circles. The Asian experts in the State Department agreed that Chiang's defeat was the result of Nationalist incompetence and corruption. They knew that Soviet support for the CCP during the civil war had been sporadic and lackluster. Many of them realized that Mao was not Stalin's puppet. But since the Chinese Communists sought to transform China's economy and society, declared their preference for the Kremlin's side in the Cold War, and abused some Americans inside China, Truman would not recognize the new regime, especially when he was being denounced for having "lost China." His administration attempted to drive a wedge between Stalin and Mao and to prevent the latter from consolidating his power. China, Truman's advisors thought, was too poor and too weak to matter a great deal, but the implications of a Chinese Communist victory for other parts of Asia were of great consequence.

Japan was seen by everyone in Washington as the key to Asia's future. Dean Acheson, Truman's choice for secretary of state after Marshall resigned, and John Foster Dulles, the leading Republican spokesman on foreign-policy issues, agreed that if Japan were added to the Soviet bloc the Kremlin would acquire the skilled labor and industrial potential to shift the balance of world power. They knew the Kremlin would not try to take Japan militarily, but they agonized over the problems of Japanese rehabilitation. For the moment, the Americans were in control of the occupation. But the occupation would not last long, because neither American taxpayers nor the Japanese people would tolerate it for long. Policymakers in Washington, therefore, worried that Japan's slow economic recovery and monumental trade deficits would impel Japanese leaders to look to the East for markets. The State and Defense departments feared that Communist successes elsewhere might suck Japan into the Soviet orbit, since Japan's sources of raw materials and foodstuffs were traditionally found in Manchuria, north China,

Korea, and Taiwan—areas already under Communist control or likely to be so in the near future.

Japan was the most valuable country in Asia because of its industrial potential and talented work force. Those assets might escape the control of the West once the occupation ended, if Japan were not firmly integrated into the Western orbit. Given the loss of China, American officials believed, Japan had to be linked to the markets and raw materials in Southeast Asia. All the different agencies in Washington agreed that this integration was essential, and so did Republican leaders like Dulles, who joined the State Department as a consultant for Asian issues.

In 1948 and 1949, however, Indonesian nationalists under the leadership of Sukarno and Vietnamese nationalists under the aegis of Ho Chi Minh were in the midst of throwing the Dutch and the French out of their countries. Should their revolutions succeed, Indonesia and Indochina might not wish to go along with American schemes. They had been occupied by Japan during World War II and they dreaded Japan's revival. Ho, moreover, was a Communist. Although he had been on good terms with the Americans during World War II, his political ideology now meant he could not be trusted. And since he was likely to receive aid from the triumphant Chinese Communists on his northern border, his prospective victory in his struggle against the French was all the more probable and all the more worrisome. Japan, in short, might be lost as a result of the Communist victory in China and the revolutionary nationalist tide in Southeast Asia.

The implications of developments in Southeast Asia were still more grave because of their ripple effect on Western Europe. If Ho's forces won in Indochina, the French would feel humiliated and the delicate internal political situation in France might take a turn for the worse. Right-wing parties might assail the center, and the Communists might exploit the crisis to serve their own interests. Even though the French government partially reformed its colonial administration and handed limited power to the former emperor Bao Dai, American officials worried that French attention and capabilities would be diverted

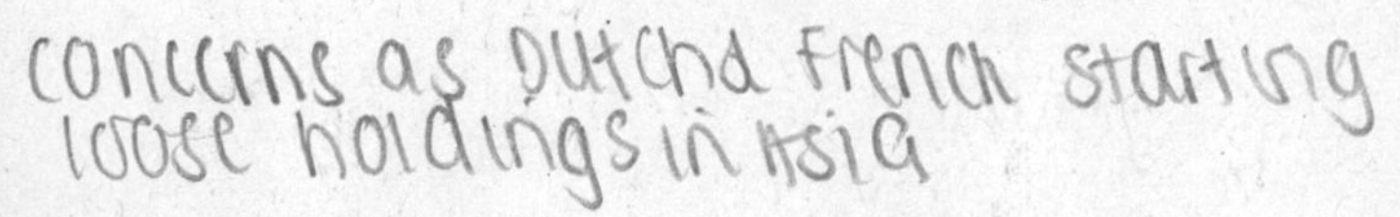

from Europe. So although U.S. officials were pleased that French troops stayed in Vietnam to battle Ho's insurgents, the strife in Indochina nevertheless endangered American desires to stabilize French politics, defeat the French Communists, and harness German power.

France's protracted struggle in Vietnam was a regrettable but necessary development to U.S. officials, because they felt that a Communist victory in Indochina would have a domino effect on Malaya and thereby do great harm to Britain. Malaya was a great exporter of rubber and tin, and the huge earnings that the British derived from the sale of these critical raw materials were of enormous importance to London's financial solvency. Mao's victory in China meant that he could aid Ho, and Ho's victory in Indochina could have a bandwagon effect on the insurgency in Malaya. Since Malaya had a large number of Chinese residents, the situation seemed especially ominous. The local Chinese could not be trusted—so American and British officials believed—because they were likely to follow the lead of the new Communist government in Peking.

These matters assumed increasing importance during the first half of 1949, because Britain faced a new sterling crisis and had to devalue its currency. In London, the devaluation of the pound triggered another agonizing reappraisal about Britain's ability to hold on to its overseas possessions. U.S. officials feared that if Britain relinquished these possessions, even more power vacuums would result.

Britain's financial duress reverberated throughout Europe. The devaluation of sterling triggered currency devaluations all through Western Europe and provoked bitter recriminations. The French were infuriated, particularly because British weakness meant that Paris might have to deal alone with the new West German state. The French were angered by Britain's reluctance to cooperate on initiatives to integrate Europe economically and were disillusioned by Britain's hesitation to commit troops and resources to support the North Atlantic Treaty.

So interwoven was the world economy and so inextricably linked were political and economic affairs that the victories in

Italy and Berlin that had seemed noteworthy in 1948 quickly lost their luster. By the latter part of the following year, U.S. officials were again lamenting the grave state of international affairs. In Western Europe, the successful completion of the North Atlantic Treaty in April 1949 was followed by interminable squabbling over the commitment of troops, the delineation of strategic plans, the allocation of military assistance, and the composition of commands. German economic growth, sparked by the currency reform, slowed down; by late 1949, there was widespread angst over the magnitude of unemployment and the lingering trade deficit. And although the French acquiesced in the formation of the Federal Republic and agreed to cede limited sovereignty to the new government, officials in Paris agonized over each and every sign of German independence, lived in dread of a resurgence of German power, and sought control over every ton of German coal.

Truman had reveled in his electrifying victory in 1948, but was quickly confronted with a worsening international situation. In his inaugural address in January 1949, he reified the ideological struggle. Communism, he declared, was a false philosophy. It enslaved the individual, glorified violence, divided the world into conflicting classes, and postulated the inevitability of war. Truman would not stand for it. He would contest it everywhere. He would promote economic recovery, strengthen freedom-loving nations against the threat of aggression, and launch bold new programs to promote technological progress and reduce poverty in underdeveloped areas.

But within months, he found himself bogged down with intractable problems abroad and a poisonous political atmosphere at home. He now faced a Communist China and revolutionary nationalist turmoil in Southeast Asia. In the Middle East, he faced an Arab world embittered by U.S. recognition of the new state of Israel in May 1948. In Western Europe and northeast Asia, he faced two ex-enemies eager to recover their full sovereignty and agitated by their economic deprivation. Yet each initiative to allay their grievances and co-opt their power set off alarm bells among former allies who were frightened by the prospect of German and Japanese revival.

During the middle of 1949 Truman's advisors started warning him again of impending paralysis in the world reconstruction process. They were worried about their ability to revive Germany and Japan, integrate Western Europe, and sustain the flow of dollars to key allies. If Marshall Plan aid terminated in 1952 and the special occupation funds dried up, how would the industrial workshops in Western Europe and northeast Asia procure the raw materials, fuel, and foodstuffs they required for their economic health and political stability? How would they then be able to finance their indispensable trade with the Middle East, Southeast Asia, and the United States? The Western alliance, Acheson was convinced, had to regain the momentum that it had grabbed after the Italian elections and the Berlin crisis.

But it was increasingly doubtful whether the United States could do so. The Soviets detonated their own atomic device in August 1949. The Russian breakthrough came earlier than expected. Alarmed, Truman asked for advice from his secretary of state, his secretary of defense, and the chairman of the Atomic Energy Commission. They urged him to build up America's atomic arsenal.

Fearful that spies might have stolen additional scientific and technological secrets, Secretary of Defense Louis Johnson and Acheson also told the president in January 1950 to accelerate work on the hydrogen bomb. If the Soviets got it first, they would neutralize the advantages that the United States had derived from its atomic monopoly. The Americans and their allies might hereafter hesitate to take risks that might provoke Russian counterthrusts. Washington, for example, might now hesitate to revive heavy industry in West Germany, or intervene in the Middle East, or sign a separate peace with Japan. Any of these moves might ignite a sequence of actions that could spiral into war, a sequence that heretofore had been avoided because the Soviets had backed down before it reached a critical stage. To regain the initiative in the Cold War, U.S. officials needed to be confident that their own strategic superiority and Western European conventional strength would enable them and their allies to deter Soviet counterthrusts.

In the early months of 1950 they did not have this confidence. Evidence accrued that the adversary was growing bolder. Mao recognized Ho's government in Vietnam, and the Kremlin followed suit. Mao then went to Moscow and signed a thirty-year treaty of mutual assistance with the Kremlin. Americans did not know of the bitter suspicions that engulfed the Mao-Stalin talks. Instead, they saw Russian military advisors and technicians flocking into China. Assistant Secretary of State Dean Rusk denounced the Chinese Communists as Stalin's "junior partners."[17] Acheson was less and less certain that he could drive a wedge between Peking and Moscow. "The Soviet Union," he said in May 1950, "possesses position of domination in China which it is using to threaten Indochina, push in Malaya, stir up trouble in the Philippines, and now to start trouble in Indonesia."[18]

The specter of a worldwide Communist movement on the march emboldened Republicans at home. They were a dour lot after their dreadful defeat in 1948. With Dewey as their candidate and Vandenberg as their foreign policy spokesman, they had endorsed a bipartisan foreign policy but had received no credit for it. In 1950, with Dewey beaten and Vandenberg dying of cancer, they were now looking for weak spots in the administration's foreign policies. They attacked Truman and Acheson for having lost China. They said it was the fault of left-leaning foreign service officers who had betrayed the Nationalists on the mainland and who were now unwilling to defend Taiwan with the use of military force. Acheson added fuel to the fire when he defended Alger Hiss after he was convicted of perjury. Hiss, a member of the East Coast foreign-policy establishment, a former State Department official, and a junior aide to Roosevelt at the Yalta Conference, was accused of passing secret documents to Soviet agents in the 1930s. His trial captivated public attention and fueled Republican allegations, mistaken though they were, that Reds dominated the State Department.

Truman had tried to deflect partisan charges that he coddled disloyal bureaucrats. He had instituted his own loyalty program, authorized the publication of a list of alleged subversive organizations, and approved FBI surveillance of suspicious individuals. But after Hiss was found guilty and Klaus Fuchs, the atomic scientist, was arrested in Britain for leaking secrets to the Kremlin, the administration was terribly vulnerable. Joseph McCarthy, the junior senator from Wisconsin, leaped into the spotlight with charges that Acheson, "the pompous diplomat in striped pants," harbored 205 Communists in the Department of State. The numbers changed almost daily, but McCarthy's message was relentless and vicious: the United States was losing the Cold War because the administration was riddled with disloyal Americans who were betraying the "Democratic Christian World."[19]

McCarthy's charges poisoned the atmosphere and further complicated policy-making. Truman, Acheson, and their advisors did believe that the country was facing serious dangers but that it was nonsense to think that the threat was domestic. In their view the threat remained what it had always been: the capacity of the Kremlin to exploit systemic weaknesses, revolutionary nationalist gains, indigenous Communist popularity, and German and Japanese despair. But the initiatives required to overcome these problems were more complicated than before, because they now entailed the rearmament of Germany, a separate peace treaty with Japan, protracted economic aid, considerable military assistance, extensive covert operations, and the indefinite deployment of U.S. forces overseas. These were all costly commitments, demanding even greater entanglements in the political affairs of Europe and Asia and necessitating sacrifices by the American people in the form of higher taxes and lower tariffs.

How could policymakers mobilize support for these measures? Paul Nitze, Acheson's trusted aide and the new director of the State Department Policy Planning Staff, seized the initiative. With his superior's full endorsement, the assistance of his staff, and the cooperation of several high officials in the Pentagon, Nitze composed one of the most important national security documents of the Cold War era. The Soviet Union, Nitze wrote in National Security Council Paper No. 68, "is animated by a new fanatic faith, antithetical to our own, and seeks to impose its absolute authority over the rest of the world." In response, the United States had to "create conditions under which our free and democratic system can live and prosper."[20] After assessing various options, Nitze said much more money had to be spent on the strategic arsenal, conventional military capabilities, military assistance, economic aid, and covert operations.

Nitze did not expect premeditated Soviet aggression. Rather, he feared that the Kremlin's growing military capabilities would inspire ever more adventurous behavior. He worried even more that Soviet atomic weapons would discourage the diplomatic, political, and economic risk-taking essential for the United States to deal with the structural economic and political problems that existed in the international system. If the necessary steps were to be taken to integrate West Germany into an American orbit, the United States would need to have the military capabilities to reassure the French and deter Soviet counterthrusts. If the United States was to have the capabilities to defend Western Europe after the Soviet atomic arsenal neutralized America's stockpile (in several years' time), it would have to build up the conventional military capabilities of its allies. If the United States was to integrate Japan and Southeast Asia, Washington had to send sufficient military assistance to friendly governments in the region. In brief, Nitze believed that expanded military strength and enhanced economic resources had to undergird the nation's foreign policy. Without such strength, U.S. options would be limited, America's potential allies would drift into neutrality, and the integrity and vitality of the American system would be endangered.

In May 1950, the Truman administration accepted NSC 68 as the conceptual framework for the conduct of its foreign policy. Acheson went to Europe to speak to Bevin and Schuman about strengthening the administrative machinery of NATO, boosting military spending, and harnessing unused West German industrial capacity for the military buildup in the rest of Western Europe. He wanted the French and the British to placate the new West German government of Konrad Adenauer.

He urged them to relax further the controls over the German economy and foreign policy. This could be done, he knew, only if it was certain that the Federal Republic of Germany was firmly ensconced in the Western alliance. Hence Acheson wanted his allies to think about admitting West Germany into NATO. Acheson knew that requests of this sort would engender acrimony. To make them more agreeable, he intimated that the Truman administration might be willing to extend aid beyond 1952.

During the spring of 1950 Acheson and his aides firmed up the U.S. position throughout the globe. With regard to the Middle East, they prodded Congress to allocate funds for the promotion of economic opportunity in areas settled by Palestinian refugees. They beseeched Congress for military assistance to Iran and Saudi Arabia, and they supported British arms sales to Egypt. They started to implement a military and economic aid program for all the countries of Southeast Asia. They recognized Bao Dai in Vietnam and began to bolster the French effort to shore up that government. And they pondered a variety of plans to dislodge Chiang from his seat of power, install another government in Taiwan, and defend the island from the Chinese Communists.

Altogether, the planning and the actions undertaken in the spring of 1950 illustrate the State Department's growing readiness to assume a position of hegemony in the international system. Acheson, Nitze, and their aides were willing to assume more and more of the responsibilities to ensure the military security and financial liquidity of the non-Communist world. They were preparing to turn the North Atlantic Treaty into a real organization; they were thinking about the permanent deployment of five U.S. divisions to Europe; they were pondering new strategies to satisfy the Germans and deflect their pleas for unity and neutrality; they were working on a separate peace treaty with Japan that would end the occupation yet retain a U.S. military presence there; they were thinking of systematizing the long-term flow of dollars overseas; and they were contemplating measures that would ensure the survival of pro-Western governments in the Middle East and Southeast Asia, the prerequisite for their successful integration with the industrial workshops of Western Europe and Japan. In all these efforts, they were fashioning techniques and strategies to collaborate with local leaders, sometimes democratically elected and sometimes not, without whose assent U.S. hegemony would not be possible.

Yet President Truman still deliberated. He agonized over the question of German rearmament. He read NSC 68, supported its conclusions, yet hesitated to endorse Nitze's desire to triple the nation's military expenditures. Although the Marshall Plan, the North Atlantic Treaty, and the occupations of Japan and Germany had transformed the international role of the United States, Truman still worried whether the mounting costs and dangers of hegemony outweighed its benefits. Sophisticated and trusted advisors like Clifford, Acheson, Lovett, Harriman, Marshall, and Nitze told him that the containment of Communism and Soviet power was essential to preserve an open world economy and democratic capitalism in the United States. But the farm boy from Missouri, the World War I veteran, the parochial senator from Missouri, the fiscal conservative from the midwest had his doubts. He still wondered whether the responsibilities and obligations entailed by hegemony might themselves impose burdens that would hurt the American economy, unnecessarily augment its military establishment, poison the political atmosphere, and undermine its democratic system. Paradoxically, the steps required to contain Soviet/Communist power and forestall a garrison state might themselves lead the United States toward becoming a garrison state.

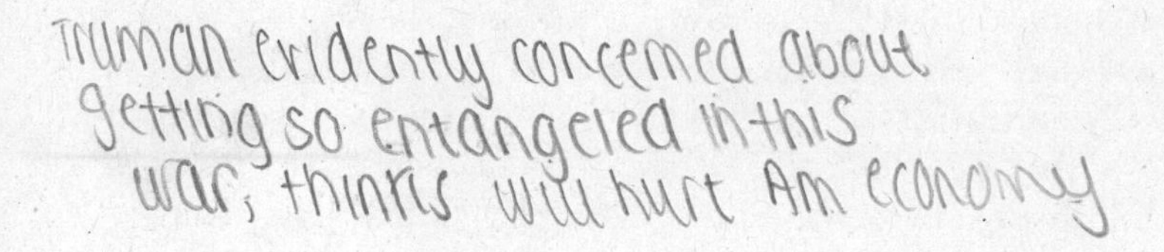

(4)

LIMITED WAR AND GLOBAL STRATEGY, 1950–1953

WHILE top American officials in Washington were deliberating on NSC 68 in April 1950, Kim Il Sung, the leader of the Democratic People's Republic of Korea, was traveling from Moscow to Peking. He was a tough, young revolutionary nationalist who had spent the war years fighting the Japanese alongside Mao's forces in Manchuria and north China. At the end of the war the Russians had moved into northern Korea and the Americans into southern Korea. With the help of Soviet occupation forces and with considerable indigenous support, Kim assumed power in North Korea and maintained it after Soviet troops left in 1948. Kim longed to unify all of Korea under his Communist rule. He detested the Japanese and abhorred American attempts to revive the former colonial master of his own people.

In Moscow Kim pressed Stalin for his approval to use North Korean military force to unify the peninsula. Stalin was not an eager accomplice, but Kim stressed that his superior forces could quickly overwhelm the opposition. He also said that there would be a massive uprising of Communist supporters in the south. Kim believed that the Americans would not have time to intervene and that his forces would triumph in less than a month.

Stalin may have doubted this assessment. According to one recent account, he warned Kim, "If you should get kicked in the teeth, I shall not lift a finger." But at the same time Stalin did not want to be viewed as the opponent of another revolutionary movement in Asia. The previous year he had awkwardly apologized to the Chinese for his meager support of their long-term struggle. Knowing that Mao already had agreed to the return of another 25,000 Korean troops who had fought with the Chinese People's Liberation Army, Stalin promised Kim the military assistance he would need. During May and June, supplies flowed into North Korea from the Soviet Union, and Russian military advisors worked with the North Koreans on their war plans. If Kim's forces succeeded, Stalin would hope to expand the buffer zone along his border, improve the Kremlin's strategic position vis-à-vis Japan, preserve Communist solidarity in Asia, and divert American power from Europe.

After leaving Moscow, Kim went to Peking to speak to Mao. Kim apparently talked in vague terms about the forthcoming attack, and may have exaggerated Stalin's endorsement in order to obtain Mao's approval. The Chinese worried that Korean actions might provoke American countermeasures that could interfere with their struggle to seize Taiwan and to put an end to the Nationalist resistance. But they could not oppose Kim's desire to unite his country. He had been a fellow comrade in arms, and his aspirations coincided with their own.

On June 25, 1950, North Korean troops attacked the south. News of the invasion triggered alarm bells in Washington. Truman and his advisors hurriedly gathered in the capital for a series of tense meetings and decided to seek a United Nations resolution denouncing the attack. When this had no effect, the president ordered American air power based in Japan to slow down the North Korean advance. He also instructed General Douglas MacArthur, commander in chief of U.S. forces in the Far East and the head of the American occupation government in Japan, to deploy two understaffed American divisions to assist South Korean armies. The administration then secured a second United Nations resolution calling for the restoration of the territorial status quo, the division of Korea between the north and the south at the 38th parallel.

Truman and Acheson were determined to stop the aggression. In their eyes this was a test case of their will. They had no doubt

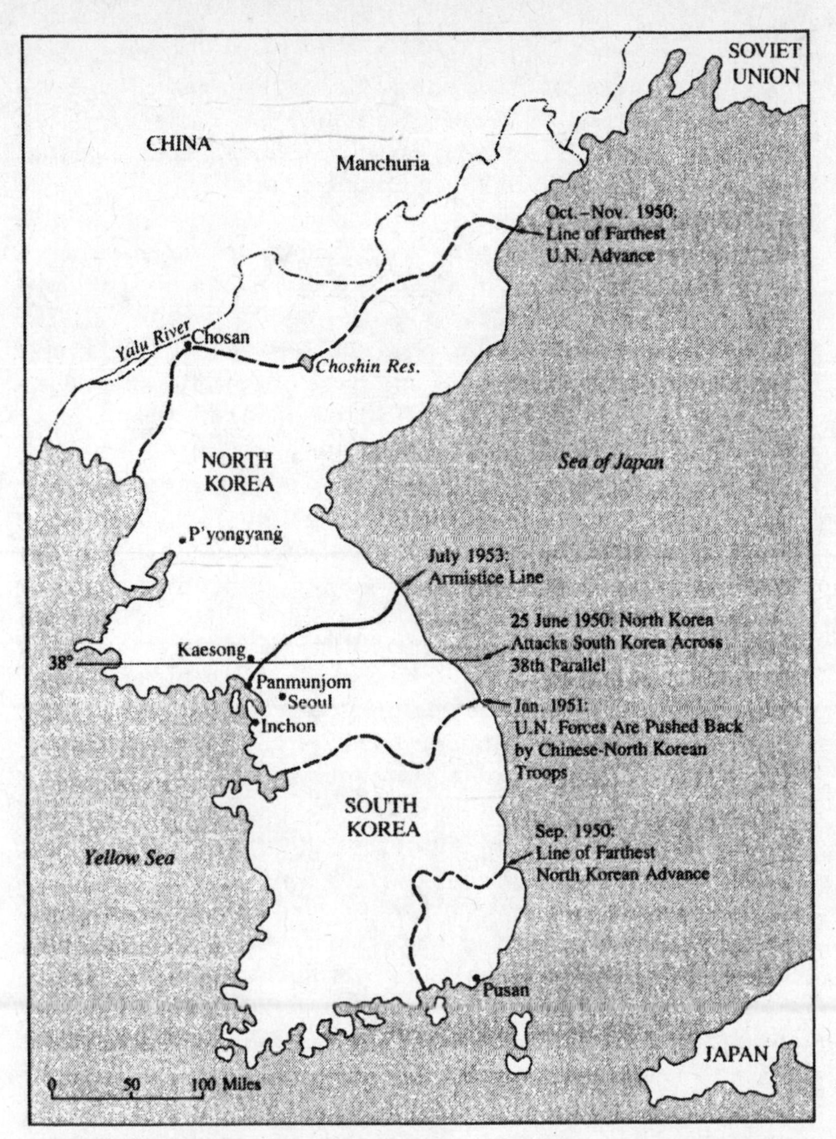

7. THE KOREAN WAR, 1950–1953

Reprinted from *An Interpretive History of American Foreign Relations*, (Homewood, Ill.: The Dorsey Press, 1968), with the permission of Wayne Cole

that the Soviets inspired the attack. Korea, Truman told one of his close associates, "is the Greece of the Far East. If we are tough enough now, if we stand up to them like we did in Greece three years ago, they won't take any next steps."[2]

U.S. policymakers felt they had to intervene. Inaction would destroy the credibility of American commitments and encourage neutralism. America's allies would lose faith in the United States, and the Germans and Japanese would doubt America's will. "If we let Korea down," Truman stressed, "the Soviet [sic] will keep right on going and swallow up one piece of Asia after another. . . . If we were to let Asia go, the Near East would collapse and no telling what would happen in Europe."[3]

Korea was of peripheral interest, but its significance was great. The United States had occupied its southern part in September 1945 to arrange the surrender of Japanese troops. With the acquiescence of the Kremlin, Washington established its own occupation regime in the south. Although Koreans longed for independence after suffering four decades of Japanese rule, the Truman administration feared that a quick withdrawal would allow radical nationalists or Communists to take control. Fearing that this would redound to the advantage of the Soviet Union, General John Hodge, the American military governor, chose to rely on conservative elements and former Japanese collaborators to establish order in the midst of widespread unrest and economic hardship.

Very quickly American officials decided that Korea was a heavy liability that diverted resources from more important places. In 1948 they formed a government in South Korea under Syngman Rhee, a conservative authoritarian nationalist who aspired to unite all of Korea under his own auspices. After Soviet troops pulled out of the north, American occupation forces left the south. The Joint Chiefs of Staff stated that Korea was not vital in wartime. In a famous speech in February 1950, Secretary of State Acheson said it was not part of America's defense perimeter. Many observers, and perhaps Kim, Mao, and Stalin, thought that the Truman administration was writing off Korea. They were wrong.

In fact, the American withdrawal from Korea had always been hedged. Although U.S. troops were in greater demand elsewhere, officials had emphasized that they must manage withdrawal "without abandoning Korea to Soviet domination."[4] Before he left office in January 1949 Secretary of State Marshall built up South Korean forces. Wanting these men to be well trained, he provided American military advisors, military assistance, and economic aid. In January and February 1950, Acheson waged a tenacious battle with Republicans in Congress to continue assistance to Korea. And while the Joint Chiefs of Staff were prepared to abandon Korea in time of global war, the Army designed plans to defend it in times of cold peace. When Acheson excluded Korea from the nation's defense perimeter, he was referring to strategic thinking about what the United States would do in case of a general war, not what he would do in case of a limited probe or local aggression. Indeed, he had said that he would call for collective action should South Korea be threatened in peacetime.

Although peripheral, Korea was not viewed as inconsequential, at least not by Truman and Acheson. Their global vision made a defense in Korea imperative. Their decision to intervene militarily was dictated by their perception of threat and their conception of Cold War global strategy. The Soviets were on the march, emboldened by the triumph of the Communists in China and their own acquisition of atomic capabilities. They had to be stopped in the periphery lest a triumph there erode American power in the industrial core.

Truman acted through executive fiat. He did not request support from Congress. When Senator Kenneth Wherry, the Republican floor leader, asked Truman why he had not consulted Congress, Truman replied that there had been no time. In fact, Republicans had shown scant interest in Korea. Had the administration not acted, they would have excoriated Truman for having lost another outpost in East Asia. But they certainly did not constitute a groundswell of support for intervention in Korea; their eyes were on China.

The administration's eyes were on the Kremlin. Truman and

Acheson were unaware of the instrumental role Kim himself had played in initiating the conflict. Ignorant of the North Korean leader's intense nationalism and unaware of the complex interaction between the North Koreans, the Chinese Communists, and the Russians, they did not believe that Kim had the capacity to shape events. Yet although Truman and Acheson were certain that the Soviet Union had inspired the attack, they were also sure that the Kremlin did not want war. General Omar Bradley, the chairman of the Joint Chiefs of Staff, and Admiral Forrest Sherman, the chief of naval operations, told Truman that they did not believe Stalin was ready for global conflict. Nor did the U.S. ambassador in Moscow. Kennan, now the counsellor in the State Department, confirmed this assessment, as did the head of the Central Intelligence Agency (CIA).

We now know, in fact, that Stalin was surprised by the American intervention and immediately took action to avoid a great power conflict. The Kremlin did not want Soviet military advisors or ships or citizens to become involved in the war for fear that it would serve as a pretext for a U.S. strike against the Soviet Union itself. Russian military advisors were withdrawn from the front and Soviet ships that had sailed to the war zone were ordered to return to port. In late 1950 and early 1951, when Soviet air power was deployed to the region and Soviet pilots directly engaged U.S. combat aircraft, Russian pilots wore Chinese uniforms and were prohibited from flying over South Korean or Japanese territory so that they could not be taken prisoner if shot down. All accounts we now have from both Chinese and Russian sources testify to Stalin's great fear of getting embroiled in war with the United States. "Stalin backed Kim Il Sung and gave him help," Nikita Khrushchev says in the glasnost version of his recollections, "but he lacked understanding of the situation. He showed cowardice. He was afraid of the United States. Stalin had his nose to the ground. He developed fear, literally fear, of the United States."[5]

Once the initial assault was stopped and American and South Korean troops dug in around the Pusan perimeter, Truman and his aides assessed the likelihood of Soviet probes elsewhere.

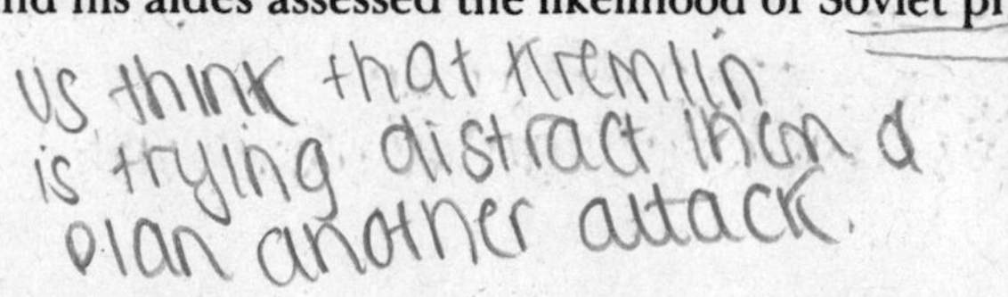

They thought the Kremlin might be acting slyly, trying to entrap the United States in a war in a marginal locale while preparing to strike quickly for something critical, perhaps Iran and the Persian Gulf, perhaps West Germany and Western Europe. But try as they did to find evidence of an imminent move elsewhere, they were unable to do so. The Kremlin was acting cautiously in the light of American superiority in atomic weapons, strategic forces, and war-making capabilities. In the middle of 1950, it was estimated that the Soviets had fewer than 25 atomic bombs and no means to deliver them against the United States. In contrast, the United States had over 500 atomic bombs, 264 nuclear-capable aircraft, and access to bases and airfields in Alaska, Canada, the Azores, the United Kingdom, Iceland, Libya, Saudi Arabia, Egypt, and Okinawa.

But Truman's advisors were also convinced that the margin of American superiority would prove fleeting if they did not use the existing situation to implement NSC 68 and expand the military capabilities of the United States and its allies. By 1952, they thought, the Soviets might have 95 atomic bombs and might believe they could inflict grievous damage on the American economy. If Western Europe could not be defended conventionally, the Soviets might feel bold enough to take more risks, thinking that the Americans would no longer try to stop them lest the United States be bombed and Western Europe overrun. If the Kremlin thought the Americans would equivocate in a crisis, Moscow might be tempted to act more adventuresomely.

The lessons, therefore, were clear. The United States must use the Korean crisis to build up its overall strength. Acheson and his aides became exasperated with the efforts of the Pentagon and the CIA to predict the Kremlin's next step; they wanted the United States to wrest the initiative and move boldly ahead. On July 19, Truman announced to the American people that he would ask Congress for an additional $10 billion to beef up U.S. military capabilities. He also wanted $260 million for the Atomic Energy Commission and an extra $4 billion for military aid to U.S. allies. Although Truman and his advisors

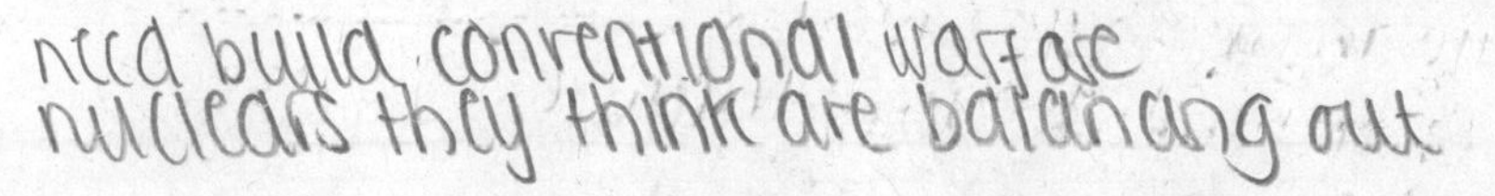

assumed the Korean War would be over by June 1951, they calculated that postwar defense budgets would be about 400 percent greater than they had previously been.

Military power was critical to support an offensive diplomacy. And during the summer of 1950 Truman and his advisors were intent on taking the diplomatic offensive and implementing their global strategy. Indeed, as soon as hostilities erupted on June 25, the president ordered the Seventh Fleet to sail into the Taiwan Strait to defend Taiwan against a prospective Communist Chinese attack. He also boosted military assistance to Indochina and the Philippines. He authorized the State Department and the Defense Department to move ahead with the preparation of a Japanese peace treaty, one that would end the occupation yet maintain an American military presence in the home islands.

More important, Truman now supported Acheson's desire to rearm West Germany and harness its industrial capabilities to NATO military plans. As for NATO itself, it had to be strengthened, given an American military commander, and buttressed with the permanent presence of four U.S. divisions. American allies would have to shift their priorities from economic reconstruction to military refurbishment. If military strength in Europe could be created, America's allies would not live in dread of a Soviet attack. Even if the growth of Soviet nuclear forces neutralized the American arsenal, the Kremlin would still have to think twice before starting a war or even threatening one. The Soviet leaders would not be able to dominate a cycle of escalation. Knowing that they could not easily overrun the European continent, they would not be able to think that they could rapidly assimilate the resources of the Old World into the Soviet command economy and war machine. The Russians would know they would be vulnerable to American counterattack, and they would think twice before taking additional adventures like the one in Korea. On the other hand, if the United States was confident that Europe could be defended with conventional forces, it would be able to act more boldly without fear of the Soviets' attacking and seizing Western Europe.

Unless the United States engaged in a military buildup and a diplomatic offensive, the correlation of forces would turn to the Kremlin's advantage. But for the moment, the United States possessed superior overall strength, and American officials decided to capitalize on it. From the early days of July 1950, Assistant Secretary of State Dean Rusk and his subordinates in the Office of Northeast Asian Affairs pondered the possibilities of moving from containment to rollback in Korea. Should the military situation improve, they wanted UN troops under General MacArthur's command to cross the 38th parallel and unify all Korea under a non-Communist government. The advantages were alluring. Penetration of the Soviet orbit, said one State Department study, "would disturb the political, economic and military structure which the USSR is organizing between its own Far Eastern territories and the contiguous areas. . . . Throughout Asia, those who foresee only inevitable Soviet conquest would take hope."[6]

Risks, of course, inhered in this strategy. Nitze and his assistants on the State Department Policy Planning Staff warned that a move across the parallel might frighten the Soviets and the Chinese and precipitate a larger war. Policymakers in Washington agreed that they had to scrutinize their adversaries to determine whether they were likely to intervene. Signs that the Kremlin wanted to negotiate actually whetted the American appetite for taking risks. On September 11, 1950, Truman agreed that MacArthur could cross the former frontier. He needed to exercise caution only if he had information that the Soviets or the Chinese might intervene. Barring such evidence, the United States would seize the offensive and move from containment to rollback.

A few days later MacArthur successfully landed his forces behind enemy lines at Inchon and entrapped large numbers of the adversary's troops. Seeing no evidence of likely Soviet or Chinese countermeasures, South Korean armies moved across the border on September 30, and the following day MacArthur demanded Kim Il Sung's unconditional surrender. Wishing to capitalize on the military momentum, the administration now decided to move from the restoration of the status quo ante to the unification of all of Korea under a non-Communist government. Acheson persuaded the United Nations to support the change in mission.

This was a decisive moment in the Korean War. Kim appealed to Mao for help. Stalin cabled Mao, telling him that he had to save Kim and promising Soviet air cover. Fearing the implications of an American presence on his own border, Mao agreed to intervene. On October 2, he informed Stalin that if China failed to act, the Korean revolutionary forces would be completely destroyed: "We will then see the American invaders more rampant, which will be very unfavorable to the whole east."[7]

Mao sent his foreign minister, Zhou Enlai, to Russia to arrange plans with Stalin. Arriving at the Soviet dictator's dacha on the Black Sea, Zhou was stunned to learn that Stalin no longer was willing to deploy Soviet air forces to Korea. Stalin said that he wanted the Chinese to fight and would give them aid, but he would not allow Soviet Russia to become directly embroiled in the war. Stalin would not fight to save Kim.

The Chinese were infuriated. Mao called his commanders back from Manchuria for another round of consultations. Zhou returned from Soviet Russia, and he, too, participated in the agonizing deliberations. Some members of the politburo did not want to intervene. They feared that intervention would spark American retaliatory actions against China, set back reconstruction, and jeopardize the success of the revolution.

Mao prevailed. He felt that China had to intervene. "If we do not send troops, the reactionaries at home and abroad would be swollen with arrogance when the enemy troops press on toward the Yalu River."[8] Mao thought that Chinese inaction would have a bandwagon effect, spurring his opponents inside China and encouraging those outside. Should the Americans be successful in Korea, they would be positioned on China's frontier, where they would then try to subvert his own regime. About three million people were still fighting against the revolution, including 600,000 Nationalists and their agents. They sabotaged communication lines and assassinated Communist officials, perhaps as many as 40,000 during the preceding months. These opponents would be greatly heartened by the destruction of the North Korean government. They would try to reverse Mao's own revolution, and they would be likely to receive American aid.

After days of excruciating soul-searching, Mao again decided on October 15 to send Chinese "volunteers" to Korea. They were to cross the Yalu River, concentrate on attacking South Korean forces, and assume a defensive posture in the mountainous region north of Pyongyang and Wonsan. Mao did not say what he would do if MacArthur himself moved quickly toward the Yalu. But when Peng Dehuai, his top general, designed a strategy to induce the South Koreans to advance forward and overextend their lines, Mao endorsed it. On October 25, Chinese troops launched an offensive against South Korean forces and pushed them back from the Yalu River. The Chinese then retreated about thirty kilometers, occupied favorable positions, and waited to see what MacArthur would do. According to their commander, they were "purposely showing ourselves to be weak, increasing the arrogance of the enemy, letting them run amuck, and luring them deep into our areas."[9]

American officials knew little of the deliberations going on in Peking and Moscow. They looked for indications that the Kremlin was preparing for war and saw few signs that Stalin intended to get involved. They also studied Chinese troop deployments and correctly observed Chinese armies moving into Manchuria. But analysts from the State Department, the Pentagon, and the CIA thought Mao was bluffing. They did not think that he would intervene in Korea, invite retaliation, and jeopardize his plans for modernizing China.

MacArthur insisted that he understood the "Oriental" mentality better than anyone, and he was sure that the Chinese would not challenge American power. Even after panicking for a moment when Chinese troops bloodied South Korean forces inside Korea in late October, MacArthur quickly regained his composure when the Chinese retreated into the mountains. His intelligence experts told him there were only about 30,000 Chinese troops in Korea, and he believed Mao was bluffing. MacArthur told Washington that he would launch the final offensive on November 24, march to the Yalu River, and defeat the North Koreans.

Top officials in Washington were not as confident as MacArthur. Although it was hard to overrule a determined commander after his display of tactical brilliance at Inchon, they still distrusted his ambitions and questioned his judgments. After agonizing deliberations, Truman and his advisors decided that MacArthur's desires comported with their own best judgments about the enemy's intentions and American interests. At a critical meeting of the National Security Council (NSC) in early November, CIA Director Walter Bedell Smith said he "saw no reason to change the previous estimate that the Soviets are not prepared themselves to bring on a general war."[10] If the Soviets were not ready to risk global war and if the Chinese were not prepared to jeopardize the success of their revolution, why not take the offensive? A sense of their own superior power infused U.S. officials with a willingness to take risks of their own.

The lure of a victory was intoxicating. "The decisive defeat of North Korean aggression and the successful unification of Korea," concluded a State Department study, "would represent a victory . . . of incalculable importance in Asia and throughout the world."[11] The British prodded Acheson to negotiate, but he refused to do so until he saw the results of MacArthur's offensive. "Defense believes, and we agree," Acheson said at the close of a critical NSC meeting, "that General MacArthur's directive should not be changed at present."[12]

MacArthur took his troops right into the trap that had been laid for him. The Chinese launched a counteroffensive and sent American forces reeling. On December 5, Chinese and North Korean troops recaptured Pyongyang, and a week later they approached the 38th parallel. Savoring unanticipated success, Mao decided to drive the Americans off the Korean peninsula. His commanders in the field warned of logistical problems and inadequate supplies. Mao overruled them, insisting that they chase the Americans south of the 38th parallel. He tasted victory as keenly as MacArthur had two weeks earlier, and his view of the bandwagon effect of a Communist victory was the mirror image of Acheson's. Mao now imagined succoring the forces of revolution throughout Asia, unifying Korea under Kim Il Sung, abetting Ho Chi Minh's cause in Vietnam, and, most of all, thwarting his opponents inside China and seizing Taiwan. While his armies marched forward in Korea, his security forces launched an attack on counterrevolutionaries at home, executing almost a million foes, jailing over a million more, and placing another million and a quarter under surveillance.

Fear gripped Washington. Acheson, Bradley, and Smith believed that the enemy would bow to American strength, and they erred egregiously. Assuming that the Chinese were acting at the Kremlin's behest, they now speculated that the Kremlin might be ready to escalate to global war. Acheson said, "Time is shorter than we thought," and Truman ruminated publicly on the possibilities of using atomic weapons.[13]

The president and the secretary of state agreed that the United States should wage a limited war in Korea. So did George Marshall, who had rejoined the administration as secretary of defense. Truman, Acheson, and Marshall concurred that the United States should neither withdraw nor escalate. If they withdrew, they assumed, much of Asia would be lost to the Communists. If they bombed China, as MacArthur insisted they should, the Soviets might be tempted to go yet another step up the escalatory spiral, attack Western Europe, and precipitate a full-scale war that everyone wished to avoid.

U.S. officials did not want to fight a major war, but they still hoped to preserve a configuration of power in the international system that comported with the needs of their domestic political economy. In January 1951, Truman put the situation bluntly to the American people: "If Western Europe were to fall to Soviet Russia, it would double the Soviet supply of coal and triple the Soviet supply of steel. If the countries of Asia and Africa should fall to Soviet Russia, we would lose the sources of many of our most vital raw materials, including uranium, which is the basis of our atomic power. And Soviet command of the free nations of Europe and Asia would confront us with military forces which we could never hope to equal. In such a situation the Soviet Union could impose its demands on the world, without resort to conflict, simply through the preponderance of its economic and military power."[14]

In order to forestall such dire consequences, American officials would now wage a limited war in Korea while pursuing their global strategy elsewhere. They would build situations of strength in the industrial core of Europe and Asia so that they could eventually regain the initiative in Korea and in other parts of the Third World periphery as well. With this additional power, they would not be self-deterred, as they now were. Nobody wanted this strength more than Secretary of State Acheson. "It would not be too much," he said at a meeting of the National Security Council on December 14, 1950, "if we had all the troops that the military want. If we had all the things that our European allies want it would not be too much. If we had the equipment to call out the reserves it would not be too much. If we had a system for full mobilization it would not be too much."[15]

But General MacArthur did not want to wait for the accretion of strength and he did not want to wage the limited war Washington officials insisted upon. In mid-January 1951, he stopped the Chinese and North Korean offensive and then counterattacked. Protracted fighting ensued somewhat south of the prewar border. But MacArthur yearned to take the war to the enemy's heartland. He wanted to blockade China, bomb Manchurian targets, and recruit Nationalist forces. He carped at Truman and heaped blame on others. He maneuvered and prevaricated to free himself from the tactical constraints. In early April 1951, Truman fired him.

Truman's sacking of MacArthur provoked a storm of controversy. The public already was disillusioned with the administration's deployment of additional troops to Europe while waging a stalemated war in Korea. MacArthur returned to a hero's welcome, and his friends in Congress conducted a full investigation of Truman's decision to fire him. Publicly, Truman could not admit the real reason: he and his military advisors in Washington were as worried as MacArthur was about the growing embroilment of Soviet air power in the conflict, and they wanted to get ready to use atomic weapons. They feared MacArthur would be too quick on the trigger. They wanted a commander in the field whom they could trust. They replaced MacArthur with Matthew Ridgway, who, since his arrival in Korea as commander of the U.S. Eighth Army, had done an impressive job.

In public hearings, the administration could not discuss the deployment of atomic weapons to the Pacific region, but Acheson, Marshall, and Bradley did lay out their diplomatic and strategic rationale in persuasive terms. They stressed that an expansion of the fighting might precipitate global conflict before they were ready for it. Time was on their side, said Acheson. The administration was building strength. Once this strength was in place, once a shield had been built in Western Europe and overriding strategic power achieved, the United States would be able to take the offensive. Right now it was imprudent to attack China directly; instead, Acheson and his aides secretly authorized covert actions, guerrilla warfare, and economic pressure. But in the future they might expand the air war as well. If the enemy bombed U.S. air and naval forces in their South Korean and Japanese sanctuaries, they would permit Ridgway to retaliate against Manchuria.

Meanwhile, Acheson and Marshall worked feverishly to build strength in Europe. They sought to rearm West Germany and lock it into a permanent Western orientation. They were fortunate that the first chancellor of the Federal Republic was the Christian Democrat Konrad Adenauer. He was firmly committed to the West, but his political position was precarious because the Social Democratic Party led by Kurt Schumacher was almost as strong as his own. Schumacher accused Adenauer of aligning too closely with the Americans, subordinating German unification, and acquiescing in protracted infringements on German sovereignty. The Americans, the British, and the French, Schumacher remonstrated, still maintained a commission overseeing the German government, still limited certain German industries, still controlled German scientific research and the direction of German trade, and still dictated its security orientation. The American plans to rearm Germany, Adenauer's other critics warned, might provoke the Russians, or expose German weakness, or tempt German rightists before democratic institutions were firmly established.

Adenauer told Acheson that much as he would like to cooperate with American demands to rebuild German forces, he could not do so unless his opponents' concerns were addressed. In particular, Adenauer requested that the allies restore German sovereignty and accept West Germany into NATO.

Justified as these requests were from the German perspective, they agitated the French. Foreign Minister Robert Schuman again told Acheson that his countrymen feared German power. Once the controls were lifted, the Germans might regain their industrial supremacy or withdraw their forces from NATO. They might negotiate with the Russians and seek unification. They might topple their own fragile democratic institutions, opt for some form of fascism or totalitarianism, and seek to regain a position of ascendancy in Central Europe. The French could not accede to American wishes and German demands unless German forces were carefully limited, integrated into a European Defense Community (EDC), and placed under foreign command.

Acting as the leader of the Western alliance, the United States sought to meet the conflicting demands of the Germans and the French. Throughout 1951 and the first half of 1952, Acheson prodded the British and the French to sign a new set of contractual agreements with Germany. In order to bolster Adenauer's position, lock Germany into a Western orbit, and effectuate its eventual rearmament, Acheson favored ending most forms of discriminatory treatment against Germany. As part of the contractual agreements, the British, the French, and the Americans agreed to abolish the Occupation Statute and the Allied High Commission. Germany regained complete control over its domestic affairs, except in times of emergency, and considerable autonomy over its foreign policy, except that it could not expel British, French, and American troops, alter its territorial boundaries, conclude a peace treaty with the Kremlin, or jeopardize Western access to Berlin. In return, Adenauer promised that West Germany would rearm, join the EDC, embrace the Western alliance structure, and forgo unilateral attempts at unification.

The United States worked equally hard to satisfy France's needs. Truman agreed to augment the U.S. commitment to French security and the NATO alliance. At the end of 1950, the president had designated Eisenhower, the organizer of victory during World War II, as the first supreme commander of NATO forces. Truman had also promised to station four divisions in Europe, notwithstanding the vicious political controversy that such a commitment provoked at home. Further, during the concluding stages of the negotiations on the European Coal and Steel Community, American diplomats had leaned heavily on the Germans to come to terms with the French. And although top military officials in the Pentagon had profound reservations about the efficacy of the French-proposed EDC, Acheson, Marshall, and Eisenhower decided to embrace this concept as an acceptable means to bring about German rearmament under the umbrella of a European army. At Schuman's request, Acheson also agreed that EDC military units would be placed under NATO's supreme commander. This organizational setup allayed French fears about the autonomy of German forces and reinforced America's leadership role in both the European and the Atlantic communities.

To reassure the French even more, the Americans agreed to limit the size and the number of German military units and to offer France lavish military aid. U.S. military units would stay in West Germany, where they could take emergency action should West Germany's democratic institutions flounder. As an effective hegemonic power exerting its leadership role, the United States co-opted West German strength and secured

Germany secure independence

German rearmament, Franco-German reconciliation, and West European integration. France still dreaded the rebirth of German power; yet Schuman got much of what France wanted: tighter security guarantees, military aid, and indirect leverage over the Ruhr industrial complex. Schuman also secured for France a position of leadership in the process of European integration.

American officials welcomed European integration, because it portended the creation of an economic unit that would encourage technological innovation and higher productivity. Enjoying economies of scale, European industries would become more competitive in world markets. If this happened, the countries of the Old World would overcome their chronic shortage of dollars and their governments would be less tempted to impose new quotas and exchange controls. The conditions for a sustained postwar recovery would be established—a recovery that would generate widespread prosperity, erode the appeal of Communist parties, and pave the way for a still more open world economy based on the free flow of capital and goods.

The American design was to create a prosperous, non-Communist Europe. Its goal was to thwart any attempt by the Kremlin to seize Western Europe in wartime, intimidate it in peacetime, or lure West Germany into its orbit anytime. To this end, Acheson encouraged European allies to double their defense spending. The United States was willing to assist them with $25 billion of military aid over a four-year period. National defense expenditures of all European NATO countries, thereafter, grew rapidly. During 1951, alliance divisions increased from 15 to 35, and operational aircraft from 1,000 to 3,000. Although the alliance never met its military goals, Eisenhower deemed the changes "prodigious."[16] No longer could the Russians think of overrunning the continent and harnessing European resources for a protracted war against the United States.

NATO was not only strengthened, it was expanded. During 1951 the United States decided to bring Greece and Turkey into the Western alliance. Some allies, like Norway and Denmark, were not happy about this expansion, but they acceded to U.S.

wishes. American defense officials wanted to be sure they could use Turkish airfields in wartime to slow down Russian armies that might head toward the Persian Gulf or the great British air base at Cairo-Suez. These same airfields could be used to strike petroleum fields in Russia and Romania. But they could not be used if the Turkish government chose to be neutral in a future conflict (as it had during World War II). And Turkish officials threatened to do just that, unless Turkey was admitted into NATO.

Building strength in Europe was only one component of the American diplomatic offensive during the Korean War. Acheson wanted to co-opt Japanese power almost as much as he hoped to co-opt German power. The Japanese were tiring of the occupation, and Acheson was worried about their loyalty. He wished to restore their sovereignty yet preserve the advantages that Japan offered the West. Defense officials in particular sought the right to keep troops in Japan wherever the Americans desired them to be stationed and for as long as the United States wanted them there. The Pentagon also hoped Japan would rearm, provide for its own defense, and gear its industries to the overall military needs of the United States and its allies.

Acheson assigned John Foster Dulles to negotiate these agreements with the Japanese prime minister Yoshida Shigeru. Yoshida was not eager to rearm. He wanted the United States to help revive the Japanese economy and to safeguard Japan's future security. Although he also sought to modify some of the occupation reforms, he was most eager to recover sovereignty over Japan's domestic life, limiting the right of American intervention to emergency situations. Yoshida was prepared to allow U.S. troops to stay as long as they desired, but he wanted to stipulate these arrangements in an administrative agreement that would not require parliamentary ratification.

American desires to end the occupation and rehabilitate the Japanese economy aroused great fears throughout Asia, much as U.S. initiatives toward Germany raised apprehensions in Europe. The Filipinos were infuriated by the prospective termination of reparation payments; the French and the British were upset by the anticipated revival of Japanese trade competition; and the Australians and the New Zealanders were alarmed by the impending re-creation of autonomous Japanese power. As in Europe, the United States had to meet the demands of these governments while simultaneously responding to the sensibilities of the Japanese.

The result was a complex network of treaties and agreements, including a multilateral peace treaty with Japan (signed in San Francisco in September 1951), a bilateral U.S.–Japan security agreement, and an administrative accord. The occupation ended and the Japanese regained control over their internal affairs. The United States guaranteed Japan's security, and in the administrative agreement the United States received wide latitude to station and redeploy its forces inside Japan. To reassure other allies in Asia and oversee the stability of the whole region, the United States signed a bilateral security agreement with the Philippines and established a loose alliance, the ANZUS alliance, with Australia and New Zealand. The United States used its power to achieve many of its key goals, but also used it to respond to the needs and entreaties of former friends and foes alike.

Yet much anxiety still persisted in Truman administration circles about the future alignment of Japan. Afraid that Japan might be sucked into the Soviet/Chinese Communist orbit through its trade relations, Acheson and Dulles made Yoshida promise to limit Japan's trade with the People's Republic of China. But knowing that before the war Japan's trade with China amounted to 17 percent of its imports and 27 percent of its exports, American officials realized that Japan could not overcome its $500 million trade deficit unless it could find markets and raw materials elsewhere. The solution, U.S. policymakers were convinced, was in Southeast Asia. If this region was "lost," Japan would have no choice but to form an "accommodation with the Communist-controlled areas in Asia."[17]

The attention of policymakers, therefore, gravitated to Indochina, where the Viet Minh was waging its war for independence against the French. Acheson aligned the United States wholeheartedly on the side of France, much as he regretted that its puppet government had no local support whatsoever. Ho Chi Minh, Acheson knew, was "the only Viet [sic] who enjoys any measure of national prestige."[18] But rather than chance another Communist victory, Acheson acknowledged that his aim was to sustain the French military effort "until the Viet Minh is liquidated and therefore no longer an effective instrument of the Kremlin and Peiping."[19]

Acheson and Robert Lovett, the new secretary of defense, were willing to expend over a billion dollars a year to keep the French fighting. Should the French leave, the United States would have to assume full responsibility for the conflict, and this would be even more costly. Beseeching Schuman to stay in Vietnam, Acheson said that if China intervened directly in the Indochina conflict, as it had in Korea, the United States would bomb China. In their last report to the president, Acheson and Lovett emphasized the need to build strength in Indochina, train Vietnamese forces, and augment the French war effort. They also stressed that the United States must develop its own capability to act militarily in the region so that it could intervene in Malaya or Indonesia, should it be necessary to do so.

While waging limited war in Korea, the emphasis on safeguarding the periphery became central to the global strategy of the Truman administration during its last year in office. The expansion of NATO, the contractual agreements with Germany, and the peace and security treaties with Japan locked the industrial core of Eurasia into an American orbit. But political turbulence, civil strife, and revolutionary nationalist movements still racked the periphery. Moscow and Peking could each exploit these circumstances to augment its own power or to weaken the cohesion and strength of America's allies in the industrial core areas of Western Europe and Northeast Asia. Consequently, Secretary of Defense Lovett persuaded Acheson that the United States should supplant British influence and assume primary responsibility for preventing Iran from falling to Communism. Warily, Acheson concluded that the United States must develop its own mobile forces to intervene in Southeast Asia and the Middle East.

Truman administration officials expected that future conflicts would occur on the periphery, and they had to be prepared to dominate any military escalation. Would the United States, questioned one member of Paul Nitze's planning staff in the State Department, still be able to "rely on threat, explicit or implicit, of global war to protect the periphery?"[20] Nitze said that it must. Time and again, he stressed that, in order to shore up the periphery, the United States had to be "willing to carry a war to the Chinese Communists and, if necessary, to the Soviet Union."[21] The aim of American policy, said Acheson, was not merely "to hold a ring around Soviet Russia. . . . Freedom of choice" must rest "with us, not the Russians."[22]

To ensure that freedom of choice, the strategic air force and the atomic arsenal grew apace. At the end of the Truman years, it was estimated that the Soviets would have about 300 atomic bombs in 1955. But given the new momentum of the American program, the United States would then have 2,250 atomic warheads, plus thermonuclear capabilities stemming from the first successful test of the hydrogen bomb in 1952. The United States also increased its strategic air wings from 21 in June 1950 to 37 in June 1952. At the same time, Air Force engineers constructed more than 100 additional overseas installations from which American strategic bombers could fly. The idea, said General Curtis LeMay, the commander of the Strategic Air Command, "was to have overwhelming strength." If the United States had it, it would then be able to "prevail at the highest level of intensity, so that any kind of an escalation would be to the disadvantage of the enemy."[23]

Along with the acceleration of America's strategic capabilities and the buildup of NATO armies in Europe, there was an immense mobilization of U.S. economic war-making capabilities, far exceeding that taking place in the Soviet Union. In early 1953, the volume of U.S. military production was seven times what it had been in June 1950. Only a small proportion of the goods were earmarked for Korea; the rest were produced to support America's global strategy in the Cold War. "Our relative preparedness for war," Nitze emphasized, determined "what initiatives we can take, when we can take them, and how far we can afford to pursue them."[24] The shadows cast across the globe by the military buildup permitted the United States to take the risks that inhered in German rearmament, the enlargement of NATO, and the consummation of the peace and security treaties with Japan.

While the limited war in Korea triggered bitter recriminations in Congress, the Democratic administration's overall global strategy won legislative approval time and again. Republicans excoriated Acheson and tormented Truman. They denounced the president's intention to deploy four divisions to Europe. In early 1951, they launched a great debate in the capitol, seeking to restrict the president's authority to move troops. But the controversy ended with a compromise resolution more or less approving what the president had already done. Republicans then remonstrated against U.S. aid to Europe. When the administration cleverly packaged its assistance in a Mutual Security Program, the Congress nibbled at the numbers yet authorized most of what Truman requested. When the administration presented the contractual agreements with Germany, the Senate approved. When the administration sent forward the peace and security treaties with Japan, the Republican John Foster Dulles defended his own handiwork and the treaties sailed through the legislature. For fiscal years 1951 and 1952, Truman asked Congress for almost $140 billion for his national security programs, and, despite congressional carping, he got most of it.

Animated by anti-Communism, Truman's enemies had difficulty posing an alternative strategy. In fact, many of them cared little about foreign policy, but they were eager to capitalize on anti-Communist impulses to achieve domestic goals or serve selfish interests, the most immediate of which was winning elections. Politicians like Richard M. Nixon initially found anti-Communism an irresistible tool to clobber political foes, win votes, discredit the New Deal, and attack the executive branch. Over time, anti-Communism took on a life of its own. Many Americans found that it helped them make sense of a complex world, a world they knew little about. Its appeal stemmed from the fact that it resonated with their fears or served their interests.

For example, in 1949, two days after Truman announced that the Soviets had detonated an atomic bomb, Billy Graham, a young, unknown preacher who was soon to become the most popular evangelist in America, warned a Los Angeles revival meeting that the city ranked high on the Soviet target list. Los Angeles, said Graham, not only was renowned for its sin, crime, and immorality, but also had more Communists than any other city in America. These Communists, Graham insisted, had "declared war against God, against Christ, against the Bible, and against all religion!" Only if Americans turned to Jesus Christ and accepted him as Savior, could the nation "be spared the onslaught of a demon-possessed communism." By mixing Communism and the devil, patriotism and redemption, Graham offered reassurance and salvation to millions of people unsettled by the anxieties of modern life and the atomic era. He also concocted an intoxicating brew that appealed to media tycoons who hated the New Deal and a strong state even more than they worried about Soviet Russia. "Puff Graham," William Randolph Hearst told his editors.[25]

People's fears of global conflict grew immensely, once the Korean War erupted and China intervened. The Soviets did have an atomic bomb, and British and American spies did filter information to the Kremlin. The Soviets did demand loyalty from foreign Communist parties, and Communists abroad did look to leadership from the Kremlin. Even liberals panicked. In California, Republican Governor Earl Warren convened a special session of the state legislature and asked for a state loyalty oath. All public employees had to promise that they were not members of organizations seeking to overthrow the American government. If they hedged, they could be investigated, and if they did not answer questions, they were likely to lose their jobs. What happened in California was a microcosm of what happened elsewhere.

The reality of limited war and the specter of expanding Communist power abroad engendered real fears at home. These apprehensions played into the hands of Senator Joseph McCarthy. The senator himself demonstrated scant interest in foreign policy. Instead, he looked for subversives at home. Few of them actually existed in the American government, but the witch-hunts he inspired enabled conservatives and traditionalists to attack liberals and radicals, labor unions and civil rights advocates, feminists and homosexuals. In the deep South, for example, Senator James O. Eastland of Mississippi accused groups like the Southern Conference Educational Fund of promoting Communism. Eastland summoned activists like Aubrey Williams and Virginia Durr before the Senate Internal Security Committee and charged them with fomenting class hatred and racial divisions. Although Eastland had no proof, investigations like his discredited the groups under scrutiny, isolated the accused activists, and undermined their effectiveness. In a similar manner, those who opposed new roles for women and who feared gays and lesbians targeted them as potential traitors or subversives. In the best-selling book *The Modern Woman,* Ferdinand Lundberg and Marynia Farnham claimed that political agents of the Kremlin used feminism to disrupt the West and erode its vigor.

Anti-Communist rhetoric dominated the public discourse of the early 1950s. Truman had initially used it to mobilize support for his foreign policies, but now his enemies latched on to it to denigrate his record. He was assailed for having lost China and for having become entrapped in Korea. Republicans charged that the Democrats had betrayed the nation's interests at the Yalta and Potsdam conferences. Traitors, Reds, and cowards had allegedly handed Eastern Europe to Stalin, sold him the atomic secrets, and then allowed him to build an iron curtain. The Democrats, Eisenhower and his followers claimed during their victorious 1952 election campaign, had followed a pusillanimous policy of containment rather than a strong, manly policy of liberation.

Yet once in office, President Eisenhower, Vice President Nixon, and Secretary of State Dulles pursued the same strategy as Truman had. Their talk of liberation in Eastern Europe meant nothing more than support of covert action and propaganda, policies that Truman and Acheson had inaugurated.

Eisenhower and Dulles did believe in rollback, but, like their predecessors, they thought it would evolve gradually from their having built strength in Western Europe and Northeast Asia, areas that would then serve as magnets to the Kremlin's satellites. The Republicans' "new look" strategy, with its emphasis on strategic air power and nuclear weapons, developed naturally from Truman's military buildup; Dulles's concepts of brinksmanship and massive retaliation followed the logic of Nitze's risk-taking mentality.

But before the Republicans could give sustained attention to these larger issues of global strategy, they had to break the stalemate in the Korean armistice negotiations. These talks had begun in July 1951, but had bogged down over the question of whether prisoners of war should be forced to return to their country. The Chinese said yes; the Americans said no. Although the United States stepped up its military pressure, attacked hydroelectric plants in North Korea, and repeatedly bombed the capital of Pyongyang, these actions did not produce a settlement.

During the 1952 presidential race, Eisenhower had said he would go to Korea if he won the election. Voters thought he had a scheme to end the fighting, but he had none. When he took office, the armistice talks continued to languish. Years later, Eisenhower and Dulles hinted that they had informed the enemy that they were going to use atomic weapons and expand the war into China. In fact, Eisenhower and Dulles appear to have been cautious about making atomic threats. Instead, they slightly modified the American negotiating position on the return of prisoners of war in order to make it more acceptable.

Whether the Chinese and the North Koreans feared additional escalation, we are still not sure. But it is abundantly clear that by the spring of 1953 they were eager for an armistice. North Korea suffered terribly from the devastating bombing and napalm raids; the Chinese were now eager to concentrate on domestic modernization. The Kremlin, in the midst of a leadership transition, supported a settlement. Syngman Rhee tried to obstruct it, but in July 1953 an armistice agreement was

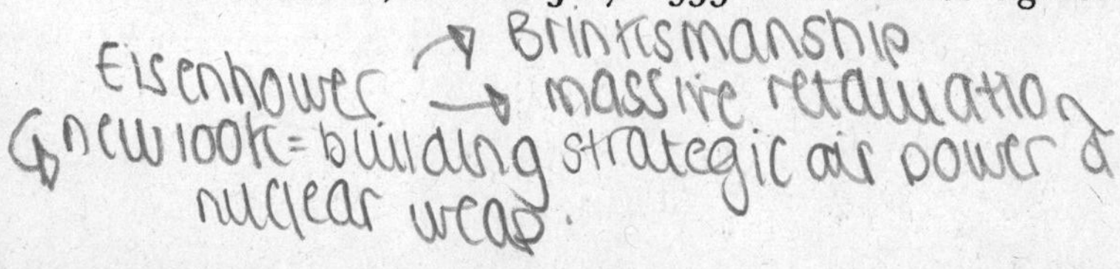

finally concluded and the prewar border reestablished. The fighting stopped; the limited war ended.

The global strategy of the United States continued. Stalin died in March 1953. The barbaric slaughterer of tens of millions of his own people was gone. His successors—Malenkov, Molotov, Beria, and Khrushchev—indicated that they were interested in relaxing tensions. They talked of peace, disarmament, and a neutral Germany. Their overtures came just as the new Eisenhower administration was getting settled in office and engaging in a thorough reassessment of U.S. diplomatic goals and strategy. The new president himself was tempted to think of a new beginning. Eisenhower gave a major speech stressing the possibilities of change. He then continued the practices of the past.

Rather than seek an end to the Cold War with a regime it did not trust, Eisenhower preferred to continue to build strength. Winston Churchill, once again Britain's prime minister, urged Eisenhower and Dulles to meet the new leaders in the Kremlin and seek some degree of understanding with them. But Ike and his advisors saw Stalin's heirs much as they had seen Stalin. American officials never had focused much attention on Stalin himself or even on his genocidal actions inside Soviet Russia. What had commanded their attention was the ability of the Soviet Union to capitalize on postwar distress in Western Europe, vacuums of power in Germany and Japan, and revolutionary nationalism in the Third World. In the view of Eisenhower and Dulles, these considerations still predominated. Although Western Europe was recovering economically, Communist parties still contended for votes and power; German and Japanese ties to the West were still considered tenuous; and decolonization and rising expectations generated more turmoil than ever before in the Middle East, North Africa, and Southeast Asia.

Given these systemic conditions, the Republicans acted much like their Democratic predecessors. Eisenhower and Dulles rebuffed the new overtures from the Kremlin and focused on containing Soviet influence and power. The international environment was too precarious to take chances. The Soviets' talk of peace might simply conceal their desire to thwart the rearmament of West Germany or to foment division within NATO. Cohesion in the Western alliance had to be preserved; German and Japanese power had to be co-opted.

Likewise, the industrial core areas of Western Europe and Japan had to be integrated with the underdeveloped periphery, and the struggle against revolutionary nationalist movements had to be sustained. In Iran, for example, Eisenhower continued the policies outlined by Lovett and Acheson in 1952. Seizing the initiative from the British, he worked covertly to overthrow the revolutionary nationalist leader Mohammed Mussadiq, thereby ensuring control of Persian Gulf oil for the reconstruction of Europe and Japan. Eisenhower also maintained the American commitment to Indochina. Although he accepted a Communist victory in northern Vietnam, he helped create a separate government in the south under Ngo Dinh Diem and gave it considerable aid. Since Dulles himself had been a principal architect of the Truman administration's policy toward Japan, it is not surprising that he continued to think that Tokyo would gravitate into the adversary's orbit if the Japanese economy was not linked to the raw materials and markets of Southeast Asia.

With the information we now have, it is difficult to know how far Stalin's successors would have gone to reach an accommodation with the West. We do know that Beria wanted to talk to the Americans and the British about a unified, neutral, and democratic Germany and that Molotov resisted the new initiative. As a result of the declassification of a fascinating set of Russian intelligence records, we also know that Soviet analysts did not think that the new administration in Washington was serious about relaxing tensions. The Kremlin saw the opening actions of the Eisenhower administration in Austria, Iran, and Afghanistan as threatening. Most important, they regarded with alarm the American attempts to rebuild and rearm West Germany, because they thought the United States would lose control over the new government.

Whatever inclination Malenkov, Molotov, and Khrushchev

may have had to reach an understanding with Washington quickly passed. Beria was killed, Molotov temporarily consolidated his authority, and Khrushchev maneuvered to gain power. The Soviets believed that negotiating on American terms would mean relinquishing their sphere of influence in Eastern Europe and accepting a powerful Germany. American conditions, they feared, would relegate the Kremlin to a position of permanent inferiority and would jeopardize the security of the Soviet state. The Kremlin preferred to sow division in the West and capitalize on the spread of national liberation movements. The men in the Kremlin took great comfort in the Soviet explosion of their first hydrogen bomb; the Russians could compete and catch up. Someday they would be able to engage in more risk-taking of their own.

From the viewpoint of Washington, there was no alternative but to continue to build a configuration of power that safeguarded American interests. For the next thirty-five years, administrations in Washington would change and tactics would vary; but the fundamental strategy would stay constant. Eisenhower's decisions in 1953 demonstrated that there would be continuity in America's global strategy no matter which party occupied the White House. By stabilizing Western Europe, coopting West Germany and Japan, and integrating these industrial core areas with the underdeveloped periphery, Democrats and Republicans alike sought to create a geopolitical configuration that comported with U.S. strategic and economic needs. This strategy constituted a double containment policy, a policy that at the same time thwarted the expansion of the Soviet Union and contained the rebirth of autonomous German and Japanese power. By integrating all non-Communist nations into an American orbit responsive to their needs and requirements, officials in Washington hoped to gain their assent to a more open and multilateral economic order, an order U.S. policymakers deemed requisite for worldwide capitalist growth and American prosperity. And if such a geopolitical and economic order could be forged abroad, it would nourish democratic capitalism at home.

This vision was a captivating one, but it wasn't certain to succeed. The Korean War, in fact, highlighted how problematic it could be. Although Truman and Eisenhower sought to create a configuration of power abroad that would preserve free markets and free men at home, the defense budget escalated beyond their expectations, a military-industrial complex came into being, and the government had to impose regulations and control prices in ways that made both presidents extremely uncomfortable. Even more threatening to democratic traditions and a free society was the new Red Scare. McCarthy's allegations of treason and his investigation of innocent individuals fostered an atmosphere of conformity at best, repression at worst.

Paradoxically, the strategy of containment and preponderance, designed to protect the core values of democratic capitalism, threatened to crush them. In the quest to enhance U.S. security, the agencies of the federal government proliferated. New ones like the CIA, the National Security Agency, and the Atomic Energy Commission came into existence, and old ones like the FBI grew in size. Under the pall of the Soviet threat abroad and McCarthyism at home, the intrusion of these agencies into people's lives mounted dangerously. The Atomic Energy Commission, for example, eager to understand the impact of radiation, secretly conducted tests on Americans, including a ten-year experiment on mentally retarded teenagers who were fed radiation-enriched cereal and other foods. State governments emulated the FBI and set up committees to probe the private lives of suspected "traitors." In Florida, for example, a committee under Charley Johns, a state senator, investigated the sexual habits of college administrators, professors, and students who were associated with the civil rights movement or who entertained African-Americans.

Many contemporaries realized that in the quest to establish a desirable configuration of power abroad and a free political economy at home, American values were being compromised, its economy overregulated, and its citizens' liberties jeopardized. Thoughtful men and women of different political persuasions worried that, in thwarting totalitarianism abroad, American governmental agencies were becoming too large and their powers too vast; the privacy, freedom, and entrepreneurship that distinguished the American way of life were being eroded. At a meeting of the National Association of Credit Men in 1950, for example, one speaker noted, "The Korean conflict has already imposed a different way of business and life upon us. What may we expect if we are called upon to fulfill our own commitments in other parts of the world? Could we, without destroying our way of life, actively discharge these obligations?"[26] And referring to foreign aid programs, a prominent financier told the American Bankers Association in 1952, "We must be careful that this does not lead to changes in the political, social, and economic organization that has made possible what we are and what we have; and does not undermine our freedoms or the sovereignty of the United States over its own affairs."[27]

As the United States became more involved in waging the Cold War and fighting the Korean War, statism, repression, and executive authority appeared to be on the rise rather than free markets and free discourse. The situation might have gotten worse if American officials had decided to prepare for a protracted conventional war, if they had opted to raise the defense budget still more, if they had implemented universal military service, or if they had insisted on full-scale defense mobilization.

But these things did not happen. Eisenhower consciously monitored developments. He did not lower defense expenditures very much, but he did constrain them. By relying on a military strategy that stressed strategic air power, he reduced the manpower requirements of the armed forces and avoided a new debate over universal military training. He also rejected comprehensive defense mobilization and governmental industrial planning, partly because these programs engendered opposition from business interests and partly because Eisenhower himself thought these things smacked of compulsory controls and regimentation. "We could lick the whole world," he noted on one occasion, "if we were willing to adopt the system of Adolf Hitler."[28] But the whole point of American policy, both foreign and domestic, was to avoid a regimented economic system and a garrison state. "I definitely believe," Eisenhower once wrote in his diary, "that the preservation of individual liberty requires what we generally refer to as a free economy."[29]

The foreign policy of the United States was designed to establish a configuration of power in the international system that nurtured free markets and personal liberty at home. During the Korean War, the McCarthy era, and the Vietnam War, this relationship was threatened but not sundered. The underlying strategy never altered: faced with the merger of Soviet power and Communist ideology, the United States sought to co-opt German and Japanese power, stabilize and integrate Western Europe, and bind core with periphery. The United States tried to act as an intelligent hegemon, or leader, seeking to establish in the non-Communist world a flourishing economy that would pull Soviet satellites westward and maybe even induce changes in the Soviet Union itself. And all this had to be done without necessitating domestic changes that would transform the United States into the garrison state that the strategy itself was designed to prevent.

The strategy was coherent, but some of the underlying assumptions were flawed. After World War II, U.S. officials had good reason to worry about the problems of European recovery, the potency of revolutionary nationalism, and the demoralization of Germany and Japan. But they exaggerated the ability of the Soviets to capitalize on these developments. Germany and Japan were not likely to gravitate voluntarily into the Soviet bloc. Nor were Communist parties in France and Italy likely to grab power, crush their opponents, betray their countries' interests, and become pawns of the Kremlin, whose armies were not in close proximity as they were in Eastern Europe. Even more questionable was the assumption that the Kremlin could shape events and control revolutionary nationalist leaders in places like Southeast Asia, a region of the world to which the United States ascribed undue importance to begin with. And most dubious of all was the belief that strategic superiority could undergird geopolitical successes in Third World areas.

Although American fears were exaggerated, they were nonetheless understandable. Should all the worst-case possibilities have eventuated, the world would have become a frightful place. Images of the 1930s resonated: totalitarian governments did seem to have a penchant for aggression. The German Nazis, Italian fascists, and Japanese militarists had waged protracted war against the United States. The Soviets were certainly totalitarian and they might do the same. Although a good case could have been made that Stalin was more prudent than Hitler in the conduct of foreign policy, no one could have been sure of it. It was not likely to happen, but if the Kremlin had capitalized on systemic weaknesses, socioeconomic dislocation, and postwar decolonization, the United States would have found itself in a more dangerous world, would have had to prepare for more ominous contingencies, and would have become more like a garrison state.

The strategy, of course, was designed to prevent these things from happening, and, ultimately, the strategy wrought victory over Soviet Communism in the Cold War. But the triumph was not without significant costs: the struggle derailed Truman's domestic reform efforts, overburdened the American economy in relation to its allies, and scarred the lives of innocent Americans targeted as Reds during the McCarthy era and as dissidents during the Vietnam War. More fatally, the Cold War meant death to more than a hundred thousand Americans fighting limited wars in Korea, Indochina, and elsewhere. And more tragically still, these so-called limited wars were total wars for the Korean and the Vietnamese peoples, who perished in the millions.

That Americans tend to forget the suffering of the Koreans and the Vietnamese is not surprising, because in waging the Cold War their principal aim was not so much to help others as to protect themselves from the specter of Communism. Thinking that geopolitical configurations were inextricably tied to economic relationships, they tried to integrate the industrial core and the Third World periphery, even while the ties were being sundered by revolutionary nationalist movements. In the view of U.S. officials, Democrats and Republicans alike, these links had to be maintained lest the power centers of Western Europe, West Germany, and Japan be weakened or sucked into the Soviet/Communist world. Should the latter occur, the Kremlin might grow strong enough to challenge the United States. The possibilities of an attack would always remain small. If, however, the Soviets gained domination over Eurasia or if there was a significant expansion of Communist influence, the United States might have to reshape its own political and economic system and become a garrison state. Hence correlations of power were seen to have profound consequences for American institutions; hence, ultimately, the Cold War was waged abroad to maintain a political economy of freedom at home.

NOTES

CHAPTER 1

1. Jane Degras, *Soviet Documents on Foreign Policy*, 3 vols. (New York: Octagon Books, 1978), 1: 20.
2. Ibid., 1: 26.
3. Ibid., 1: 34.
4. Arthur S. Link, *The Papers of Woodrow Wilson*, 68 vols. (Princeton, N.J.: Princeton University Press, 1966–1993), 45: 205.
5. Ibid., 45: 207.
6. For Trotsky's statement, see Beryl Williams, *The Russian Revolution* (Oxford, Eng.: Basil Blackwell, 1987), p. 59; for Wilson's feelings about Trotsky, see Link, *Papers*, 48: 133.
7. Link, *Papers*, 47: 422.
8. Ibid., 48: 500.
9. Ibid., 48: 497.
10. Ibid., 56: 247.
11. Ibid., 55: 314.
12. Ibid., 54: 245.
13. Ibid., 51: 350.
14. Ibid., 58: 507.
15. Francis William O'Brien, ed., *Two Peacemakers in Paris: The Hoover-Wilson Post-Armistice Letters, 1918–1920* (College Station, Tex.: Texas A & M University Press, 1978), p. 199.
16. Herbert Hoover, *The Ordeal of Woodrow Wilson* (New York: McGraw Hill, 1958), pp. 132–33.
17. O'Brien, *Two Peacemakers*, pp. 87–88.
18. Link, *Papers*, 55: 471.
19. Peter G. Filene, *Americans and the Soviet Experiment, 1917–1933* (Cambridge, Mass.: Harvard University Press, 1967), p. 59.

20. David W. McFadden, *Alternate Paths: Soviet-American Relations, 1917–1920* (New York: Oxford University Press, 1993), p. 325.
21. Degras, *Soviet Documents*, 1: 221–22.
22. Herbert C. Hoover, *The Memoirs of Herbert Hoover: The Cabinet and the Presidency* (London: Hollis and Carter, 1952), p. 182.
23. Herbert Hoover, *American Individualism* (Garden City, N.Y.: Doubleday, 1922), p. 2.
24. Degras, *Soviet Documents*, 2: 446.
25. Ibid., 2: 320.
26. M. J. Heale, *American Anticommunism: Combating the Enemy Within, 1830–1970* (Baltimore, Md.: The Johns Hopkins University Press, 1990), pp. 105–21, especially 112–13.
27. Geoffrey Roberts, "The Soviet Decision for a Pact with Nazi Germany," *Soviet Studies*, 44 (1992): 73.
28. Ibid., p. 64.
29. Beatrice Bishop Berle and Travis Beal Jacobs, eds., *Navigating the Rapids, 1918–1971: From the Papers of Adolf A. Berle* (New York: Harcourt, Brace, Jovanovich, 1973), pp. 293 and 299.
30. Samuel I. Rosenman, ed., *The Public Papers and Addresses of Franklin D. Roosevelt, 1940* (New York: Macmillan, 1941), p. 261.
31. James D. Mooney, "War or Peace in America," *Saturday Evening Post*, 3 August 1940, p. 47.
32. "The Fight for Freedom," *Fortune*, June 1941, p. 59.
33. "England Must Win, or Else—," *Reader's Digest*, January 1941, p. 57.
34. Walter Lippmann, "The Economic Consequences of a German Victory," *Life*, 22 July 1940, p. 69.
35. Arnold Offner, "Uncommon Ground," *Soviet Union/Union Soviétique*, 18 (1991): 237.

CHAPTER 2

1. Dmitri Volkogonov, *Stalin: Triumph and Tragedy* (New York: Grove Weidenfeld, 1988), pp. 409–13.
2. Milovan Djilas, *Conversations with Stalin* (New York: Harcourt, Brace & World, 1962), p. 114.
3. Sergei N. Goncharov, John W. Lewis, and Xue Litai, *Uncertain Partners: Stalin, Mao, and the Korean War* (Stanford, Calif.: Stanford University Press, 1993), p. 3.
4. Andrei Gromyko, *Memoirs* (New York: Doubleday, 1989), p. 110.

5. Nikita Khrushchev, *Khrushchev Remembers: The Glasnost Tapes*, ed. and trans. Jerrold Schecter and Vyacheslav V. Luchkov (Boston: Little, Brown, 1990), p. 69.
6. Odd Arne Westad, *Cold War and Revolution: Soviet-American Rivalry and the Origins of the Chinese Civil War* (New York: Columbia University Press, 1993), p. 55.
7. Khrushchev, *Khrushchev Remembers*, p. 72.
8. For Stalin s speech, see *Vital Speeches of the Day*, 12 (1 March 1946): 300–4.
9. For the quotation, and for an important analysis based on Soviet documents, see Scott Parrish, "The USSR and the Security Dilemma: Explaining Soviet Self-Encirclement, 1945–1985," (Harriman Institute, Columbia University, dissertation in progress), chapter 3.
10. Quoted in Martin Kitchen, "Winston Churchill and the Soviet Union During the Second World War," *The Historical Journal*, 30 (1987): 424.
11. For the quotations, see ibid., pp. 428, 431, 433.
12. Gromyko, *Memoirs*, p. 96.
13. Robert H. Ferrell, ed., *Off-the-Record: The Private Papers of Harry S. Truman* (New York: Harper & Row, 1980), p. 22.
14. Harry S Truman, *Memoirs: 1945, Year of Decisions* (New York: Signet, 1955), p. 87.
15. For the quotation, see Robert H. Ferrell, ed., *Dear Bess: Letters from Harry to Bess Truman* (New York: Norton, 1983), p. 522.
16. Ferrell, *Off-the-Record*, pp. 56–57, 45.
17. Ferrell, *Dear Bess*, p. 522.
18. Frank Roberts, "A Diplomat Remembers Stalin," *The World Today* (November 1990), p. 210.
19. Department of State, *Foreign Relations of the United States* (hereafter *FRUS*), *Conference of Berlin (Potsdam)*, 2 vols. (Washington, D.C.: Government Printing Office, 1960), 1: 61.
20. For the quotations, see Melvyn P. Leffler, *A Preponderance of Power: National Security, the Truman Administration, and the Cold War* (Stanford, Calif.: Stanford University Press, 1992), pp. 63–64, 71, 101.
21. *FRUS, Potsdam*, 1: 258.
22. Expanded draft of letter from Secretary of War to Secretary of State, "U.S. Position re Soviet Proposals on Kiel Canal and Dardanelles," 8 July 1945, ABC 093 Kiel (6 July 1945), Record Group 165, National Archives, Washington, D.C.

23. Ferrell, *Off-the-Record*, p. 80.
24. For a particularly good account of the speech and its context, see Fraser Harbutt, *The Iron Curtain: Churchill, America, and the Origins of the Cold War* (New York: Oxford University Press, 1986), pp. 185–91.
25. Arthur Krock, *Memoirs: Sixty Years on the Firing Line* (New York: Funk & Wagnalls, 1968), pp. 468–83; quotations are on 470 and 479.
26. Clark Clifford, with Richard Holbrooke, *Counsel to the President* (New York: Random House, 1991), p. 128.
27. *FRUS*, 1947, 3: 891.
28. Jean Edward Smith, ed., *The Papers of General Lucius D. Clay*, 2 vols. (Bloomington, Ind.: Indiana University Press, 1974), 1: 337.
29. Harry S. Truman, *Memoirs: 1946–52, Years of Trial and Hope* (New York: Signet, 1956), pp. 124–25.
30. *Public Papers of the Presidents: Harry S. Truman, 1947* (Washington, D.C.: Government Printing Office, 1963), pp. 170–71.
31. President's Committee on Foreign Aid, *European Recovery and American Aid* (Washington, D.C.: Government Printing Office, 1947), pp. 18–19.
32. Ibid., pp. 21–22.
33. *Public Papers of the Presidents: Truman, 1947*, pp. 176–80.
34. Quoted in Ann G. Rollow, "World War II and Wall Street's Fear of Creeping Collectivism," (University of Virginia, undergraduate honors thesis, 1992), p. 47.
35. Quoted in Rebecca Benson Pels, "The Coalescence of a Cold War Consensus: The Evolution of Fears Regarding the Soviet Union as Expressed in Selected Popular Magazines, 1944–1947" (University of Virginia, Master's thesis, 1990), p. 88.
36. Anna Kasten Nelson, ed., *Department of State Policy Planning Staff Papers*, 3 vols. (New York: Garland, 1983), 2: 78–79.
37. For Knowland's speech, see *Appendix to the Congressional Record*, vol. 93, p. A4915.
38. *Saturday Evening Post*, 13 April 1946, p. 136.
39. Council of Economic Advisers, *The Impact of Foreign Aid on the Domestic Economy* (Washington, D.C.: Government Printing Office, 1947), pp. 30–31.
40. President's Committee on Foreign Aid, *European Recovery*, p. 22.
41. Will Clayton, "Is the Marshall Plan 'Operation Rathole'?" *Saturday Evening Post*, July/August 1947, p. 27.

42. *FRUS*, 1947, 3: 476.
43. *Public Papers of the Presidents: Truman, 1952–1953*, p. 189.
44. Dean G. Acheson, *This Vast External Realm* (New York: Norton, 1973), p. 19.

CHAPTER 3

1. Letter from Novikov to Molotov, in Galina Takhnenko, "Anatomy of a Political Decision: Notes on the Marshall Plan," *International Affairs* (Moscow) (July 1992): 118–21.
2. Ibid., p. 122.
3. Scott D. Parrish, "The Turn Towards Confrontation: The Soviet Reaction to the Marshall Plan, June 1947," paper delivered at the Conference on New Evidence on Cold War History (Moscow, 1993), p. 28.
4. Dmitri Volkogonov, *Stalin: Triumph and Tragedy* (New York: Grove Weidenfeld, 1991), p. 531.
5. Kennan to Robert Lovett, October 6, 1947, box 33, Policy Planning Staff Papers, Record Group 59, National Archives.
6. Department of State, *Foreign Relations of the United States* (hereafter *FRUS*), 1947, vol. 3 (Washington, D.C.: Government Printing Office, 1972), pp. 404–5.
7. U.S. Senate, Committee on Foreign Relations, *European Recovery Program* (80th Congress, 2nd Session), p. 478.
8. *FRUS*, 1947, 3: 476.
9. Quoted in Robert Freeland, *The Truman Doctrine and the Origins of McCarthyism: Foreign Policy, Domestic Politics, and Internal Security, 1946–1948* (New York: Alfred A. Knopf, 1972), p. 196.
10. Memorandum for the President, by Clifford, October 3, 1947, Clark Clifford Papers, Harry S. Truman Library (Independence, Missouri).
11. Minutes of the National Security Council, February 12, 1948, Record Group 273, National Archives.
12. *FRUS*, 1948, vol. 1 (Washington, D.C.: Government Printing Office, 1976), p. 516.
13. Admiral Richard Conolly to Forrestal, December 19, 1947, box 19, CD 6-1-45, Record Group 330, National Archives.
14. *Public Papers of the Presidents: Harry S. Truman, 1948* (Washington, D.C.: Government Printing Office, 1964), p. 189.

15. Poster in the archives of the University of Virginia Development Fund, 1947/48, Alderman Library (Charlottesville, Virginia).
16. Quoted in John H. Backer, *Winds of History: The German Years of Lucius DuBignon Clay* (New York: Van Nostrand Reinhold, 1983), p. 229.
17. *FRUS*, 1950, vol. 6 (Washington, D.C.: Government Printing Office, 1976), p. 349.
18. Ibid., 1950, vol. 3 (Washington, D.C.: Government Printing Office, 1977), p. 1038.
19. David Oshinsky, *A Conspiracy So Immense: The World of Joe McCarthy* (New York: Free Press, 1983), p. 108.
20. Thomas H. Etzold and John Lewis Gaddis, eds., *Containment: Documents on American Policy and Strategy, 1945–1950* (New York: Columbia University Press, 1978), pp. 385–86.

CHAPTER 4

1. Sergei N. Goncharov, John W. Lewis, and Xue Litai, *Uncertain Partners: Stalin, Mao, and the Korean War* (Stanford, Calif.: Stanford University Press, 1993), p. 145.
2. Notes of George Elsey, 26 June 1950, box 71, George M. Elsey Papers, Harry S. Truman Library (Independence, Missouri).
3. Ibid.
4. Department of State, *Foreign Relations of the United States* (hereafter *FRUS*), 1947, vol. 6 (Washington, D.C.: Government Printing Office, 1972), p. 738.
5. Nikita Khrushchev, *Khrushchev Remembers: The Glasnost Tapes*, ed. and trans. Jerrold Schecter and Vyacheslav V. Luchkov (Boston: Little, Brown, 1990), p. 147.
6. *FRUS*, 1950, vol. 7 (Washington, D.C.: Government Printing Office, 1976), p. 620.
7. Quoted in Jian Chen, "The Sino-Soviet Alliance and China's Entry into the Korean War" (Washington, D.C.: Woodrow Wilson International Center, paper of the Cold War International History Project, 1991), p. 27.
8. Goncharov, Lewis, and Litai, *Uncertain Partners*, p. 181.
9. Jian Chen, "China's Changing Aims During the Korean War, 1950–51," *The Journal of American-East Asian Relations*, 1 (1992): 25.
10. Summary of National Security Council Discussion, November 10, 1950, Record Group 273, National Archives.

11. *FRUS*, 1950, 7: 655–56.
12. Summary of NSC Discussion, November 10, 1950, Record Group 273.
13. Memorandum, by Elsey, November 28, 1950, box 72, Elsey Papers.
14. *Public Papers of the Presidents: Harry S. Truman, 1951* (Washington, D.C.: Government Printing Office, 1965), p. 8.
15. Summary of NSC Discussion, 15 December 1950, Record Group 273.
16. Louis Galambos, ed., *The Papers of Dwight D. Eisenhower*, vol. 12 (Baltimore, Md.: The Johns Hopkins University Press, 1989), p. 847.
17. *FRUS*, 1952–1954, vol. 14 (Washington, D.C.: Government Printing Office, 1985), p. 1303.
18. *FRUS*, 1951, vol. 6 (Washington, D.C.: Government Printing Office, 1977), pp. 384–85; Memorandum of Conversation, by Acheson, 9 January 1951, box 66, Dean Acheson Papers, Truman Library.
19. U.S. Senate, Committee on Foreign Relations, *Executive Sessions of the Senate Foreign Relations Committee*, vol. 4 (82nd Congress, 2nd Session), p. 151.
20. *FRUS*, 1952–1954, vol. 2 (Washington, D.C.: Government Printing Office, 1984), p. 16.
21. Ibid., vol. 12 (Washington, D.C.: Government Printing Office, 1984), p. 31.
22. Ibid., p. 183.
23. Quoted in Richard H. Kohn and Joseph P. Harahan, eds. "U.S. Strategic Air Power, 1948–1962," *International Security*, 12 (1988): 89.
24. *FRUS*, 1951, vol. 1 (Washington, D.C.: Government Printing Office, 1979), p. 233.
25. Quoted in Stephen J. Whitfield, *The Culture of the Cold War* (Baltimore, Md.: Johns Hopkins University Press, 1991), pp. 76–81.
26. Quoted in Lodge Gillespie, "Dollars and Dominoes: Rhetoric and Reality in Corporate America's Perception of Southeast Asia, 1950–1961," (University of Virginia, Master's thesis, 1993), p. 20.
27. Ibid., pp. 21–22.
28. Quoted in Aaron Friedberg, "Why Didn't the United States Become a Garrison State?" *International Security*, 16 (1992): 124.
29. Quoted in Dudley Goar, "A Chance for Peace: The Eisenhower Administration and the Soviet Peace Offensive of 1953," (University of Virginia, Master's thesis, 1993), p. 10.

Recommended Reading

Acheson, Dean G. *Present at the Creation: My Years at the State Department.* New York: Norton, 1969.

Bullock, Allen Louis Charles. *Ernest Bevin: Foreign Secretary, 1945–1951.* New York: Oxford University Press, 1983.

Cumings, Bruce. *The Origins of the Korean War.* 2 vols. Princeton, N.J.: Princeton University Press, 1981, 1990.

Freeland, Richard M. *The Truman Doctrine and the Origins of McCarthyism.* New York: Knopf, 1970.

Gaddis, John Lewis. *The United States and the Origins of the Cold War, 1941–1947.* New York: Columbia University Press, 1972.

Goncharov, Sergei N., John W. Lewis, and Xue Litai. *Uncertain Partners: Stalin, Mao, and the Korean War.* Stanford, Calif.: Stanford University Press, 1993.

Harbutt, Fraser. *The Iron Curtain: Churchill, America and the Origins of the Cold War.* New York: Oxford University Press, 1986.

Heale, M. J. *American Anticommunism: Combating the Enemy Within, 1830–1970.* Baltimore, Md.: The Johns Hopkins University Press, 1990.

Hogan, Michael J. *The Marshall Plan: America, Britain, and the Reconstruction of Western Europe, 1947–1952.* New York: Cambridge University Press, 1987.

Kennan, George F. *Memoirs (1925–1950).* New York: Bantam, 1967.

———. *Soviet-American Relations, 1917–1920.* 2 vols. Princeton, N.J.: Princeton University Press, 1956–58.

Kolko, Gabriel, and Joyce Kolko. *The Limits of Power: The World and United States Foreign Policy, 1945–1954.* New York: Harper & Row, 1972.

Leffler, Melvyn P. *A Preponderance of Power: National Security, the Truman*

Administration, and the Cold War. Stanford, Calif.: Stanford University Press, 1992.

Levin, N. Gordon. *Woodrow Wilson and World Politics*. New York: Oxford University Press, 1968.

Mayer, Arno J. *Political Origins of the New Diplomacy, 1917–1918*. New Haven, Conn.: Yale University Press, 1959.

McFadden, David W. *Alternate Paths: Soviet-American Relations, 1917–1920*. New York: Oxford University Press, 1993.

Schaller, Michael. *The American Occupation of Japan: The Origins of the Cold War in Asia*. New York: Oxford University Press, 1985.

Ulam, Adam B. *Stalin: The Man and His Era*. New York: Viking Press, 1973.

Volkogonov, Dmitri. *Stalin: Triumph and Tragedy*. New York: Grove Weidenfeld, 1991.

Whitfield, Stephen J. *The Culture of the Cold War*. Baltimore, Md.: The Johns Hopkins University Press, 1991.

Index